how to find your
happy place

quiet spaces and journal pages
for busy minds

ALISON DAVIES

An Hachette UK Company
www.hachette.co.uk

First published in Great Britain in 2022 by Pyramid,
an imprint of Octopus Publishing Group Ltd
Carmelite House
50 Victoria Embankment
London, EC4Y 0DZ
www.octopusbooks.co.uk

Distributed in the US by
Hachette Book Group
1290 Avenue of the Americas
4th and 5th Floors
New York, NY 10104

Distributed in Canada by
Canadian Manda Group
664 Annette St.
Toronto, Ontario, Canada M6S 2C8

ISBN: 978-0-7537-3496-4

A CIP catalogue record for this book is available from
the British Library

Printed and bound in China

10 9 8 7 6 5 4 3 2 1

Publisher: Lucy Pessell
Designer: Hannah Coughlin
Editor: Sarah Kennedy
Editorial Assistant: Emily Martin
Senior Production Manager: Peter Hunt

Contents

Introduction

Where is your happy place? Is it somewhere far away, relaxing on a golden strand of beach, with the scent of coconut in the air? Perhaps it's closer to home, at the heart of your family, cocooned in laughter and love. It could be just a fragment in time, a memory you hold dear and revisit whenever you need to escape, or a quiet moment, sitting in your garden, safe, tranquil, detached from the world. Wherever it is, it is sacred to you; a unique space that you can go to recharge, regroup and simply be.

We all have a happy place even if we can't instantly bring it to mind. Sometimes we need a little help to get there, some encouragement to picture it, a few carefully crafted words to conjure the image and feel of the place. And sometimes we need to switch things up, change our happy place to reflect our daily needs, for while we might want joy or a sense of hope one day, on another day, we might seek forgiveness or strength to move forward. Sometimes we may turn to nature for inspiration – the sound of trees swaying in the wind or the rhythmic ebb and flow of waves against the shoreline can have a wonderfully soothing effect.

Whether you're looking for inspiration, some help to find your happy place or just a general pick-me-up, this book has all the answers. With fifteen themed happy places on offer and a selection of suggestions to enhance the meaning of each one, based upon sound, scent and touch, you have all the tools you need to begin your adventure.

To make it easier for you to transport yourself to every destination, each happy place is presented in the form of a short visualization, which includes sensory prompts to engage your imagination. When you visualize a location or situation, you immerse yourself fully, stepping into the picture and experiencing it as if you're really there. You engage your emotions, and this helps you get the most out of the narrative, and while it might take practice, over time, it becomes easier to see and be in the moment. This, coupled with the sensory suggestions, will help you connect with the theme at a deeper level. In addition, you'll find a creative exercise which captures the spirit of the happy place, and mantras and quotes to inspire you. There is also journaling space within each section for you to jot down your reflections, along with prompts and questions designed to get you thinking.

You can choose to read from cover to cover, dip in and see where the pages fall; or pick a happy place depending on what you're looking for; there are no set rules. Most importantly, this book is a guide. It encourages you to take some time out, relax and daydream a little, for with self-care and love, you'll discover your happy place has always been a part of you.

Strength

We all face challenging times in our life, and it can be hard when we're struggling to find the strength we need to move forward. Resilience is something we build over time, and while it can be difficult to remain positive when the going gets tough, it helps if we can draw upon inner reserves of strength.

Having the courage to face your fears and stand tall might sound like an extreme feat, particularly when you're in the middle of a stressful situation, but it is possible to foster the fortitude you need. Carving out time for self-care will help, along with setting boundaries and strengthening your connection to the earth. This is physically and mentally grounding, and will help you feel anchored. If you look to nature, you will see examples of strength at every turn, which you can use as inspiration.

This section aims to foster a sense of strength and tenacity, and help you step into your power every single day.

> "BE SURE YOU PUT YOUR FEET IN THE RIGHT PLACE,
> THEN STAND FIRM."
> Abraham Lincoln

What makes you feel strong? Write down a time when you felt at your strongest, and describe the experience.

....

....

....

....

....

....

....

....

....

....

....

....

....

....

What makes you feel vulnerable? List the things that make you feel weak. Think about why they make you feel this way.

What would help you remain strong when you're feeling anxious?

....

....

....

....

....

....

....

Your happy place visualization to

infuse you with power and strength

You stand at the centre of a woody enclave, in the deepest, darkest part. Gnarled trees weave above you, creating a criss-cross pattern. There is moss underfoot, it is damp and earthy smelling, as if you've just missed a sudden downpour. The cold air clings to your skin, awakening your senses. A sturdy oak groans and creeks in the breeze. It sounds like it is speaking to you, calling your name. You gaze up into the network of boughs, and then lean back with your spine against the rough bark of the tree. The darkness is comforting, and you feel like you have come home. You lengthen your body and let your torso extend like the trunk that supports you. Energy floods your system, and you feel strong, rooted in power.

Your feet press against the forest floor. You can feel them sinking deeper into the earth, fixing you to the spot.

You draw in a deep breath and feel it surging up through your legs, infusing you with renewed vigour.

You stand tall, strong and at one with nature.

"MY CORE IS STRONG AND CENTRED"

How did it feel to visualize
yourself leaning up against,
and being supported
by, the tree?

....

....

....

....

....

....

....

....

....

....

....

....

....

....

Is there anyone in your life,
who you might consider a
role model for strength?
This could be someone
you know or look up to.

What qualities do you think
they have that give them
extra strength?

....

....

....

....

....

....

> **"YOU HAVE POWER OVER YOUR MIND –
> NOT OUTSIDE EVENTS. REALIZE THIS, AND YOU
> WILL FIND STRENGTH."**
> Marcus Aurelius

The sounds of nature can be restorative and help you engage with the present moment. They can also strengthen your connection to the earth, which helps you to feel grounded. Think of the sound of the wind as it blows through the trees, the rustling of leaves upon each branch. It doesn't matter how hard the wind blows, the tree remains a stoic presence, able to bend and twist into each gust.

Find a place outside that you can go and stand among the trees. Relax and listen, imagine you are recording everything you hear so that you can recreate it in your mind, whenever you run through the visualization.

What other sounds in nature make you feel strong and invigorated?

....

....

....

....

....

....

....

....

....

....

"ONLY THE GENTLE ARE EVER REALLY STRONG."
James Dean

The rich musky smell of the earth is a powerful intoxicating scent filled with promise. While it's hard to recreate the moist woodiness that you might encounter in a dense patch of woodland, think about other scents that make you feel strong. The aroma of a hearty meal, which you know will nourish you, the sweet scent of your favourite flower in bloom. Close your eyes and imagine you're inhaling your favourite fragrance, the one that makes you feel strong and confident.

List five "strong and powerful" smells. These can be from nature, things you encounter every day, or more exotic aromas.

....

....

....

....

....

....

....

....

....

....

Think of ways in which you can enjoy these scents more often, for example taking a scented bath, or spending time in your garden...

The earth underfoot is solid, nurturing and supportive. Whether we stand on it or dig our fingers in deep and plant within the soil, there is something nourishing about the feel of each grain of dirt. According to science, it's also good for us. The microbiomes in soil can increase levels of serotonin, which naturally lift the mood and ease anxiety. They also improve our general immunity, making us feel good inside and out.

Find a patch of soil or fill a pot or planter with compost and dig in deep with both hands. Let the dirt run through your fingers and spend a few minutes kneading the soil. Use this as an opportunity to plant something, whether you're sprinkling flower seeds, popping in a bulb or planting a seedling. Pat down the earth and notice how strong it becomes at your touch.

What kind of physical activity do you do that helps you to feel strong? Walking, swimming, gardening?

....

....

....

....

....

....

....

....

....

....

....

....

....

Make a list of things you could do in nature to boost strength and vitality, for example take a hike through the countryside, ride a bike, go running.

Working on your physical, emotional and mental strength will help you develop an inner well of resilience, so it's a good idea to build exercises into your daily routine that combine all three of these aspects. You don't have to choose anything complicated. A simple activity that allows you to move, breathe and focus your mind is effective and will help to strengthen your core.

Practise this exercise at least once a day,
either in the morning or the evening.

1. Stand with your feet hip-width apart and roll your shoulders back.
2. Tilt your chin upward slightly and lengthen your spine.
3. Drop your weight down into your legs and feet and bounce lightly.
4. Take a deep breath in, count for four beats, and extend your arms straight up.
5. As you exhale, bring your arms down in a wide circular movement until they are at your sides.
6. Stand up straight and tighten your tummy muscles. You should feel a slight tug inside as your core strengthens.
7. Repeat the exercise, dropping your weight, drawing breath, then extending your arms out and down in a circular movement as you exhale, and drawing in your stomach muscles at the end.
8. Repeat another three or four times, and to finish, draw your attention to the base of your spine. This is the root chakra, an energy centre that is associated with strength and security.
9. Imagine a red ball of energy at the base of your spine getting bigger and brighter with every breath.
10. Take a long breath in, and as you do, draw the ball of energy up your spine, until it fills your entire body with warmth and power.

How did the exercise help you to feel stronger?

....

....

....

....

....

....

....

....

Which movements did you find the most effective?

....

....

....

....

....

....

....

....

....

Build upon this exercise – think of three more movements that
you could do to feel physically stronger, like jumping up and
down or running on the spot.

Now think of three things you could do to feel emotionally
stronger, for example, taking a deep breath as you stretch.

your mantra for **strength**

"I BECOME STRONGER, BRIGHTER AND MORE VIBRANT
EVERY DAY."

Use this space to record how you plan on achieving a
sense of strength in the future.

....

....

....

....

....

....

....

....

....

....

....

....

....

....

....

....

....

Happiness

We all want to be happy. It's the eternal quest, and it can often feel just out of our reach, but the reality is that we all have the ability to feel joy. It is, after all, a choice, and while it might be hard to maintain an ecstatic state all the time, it is possible to achieve a sense of satisfaction with where you are in your life right now.

Appreciating the little things that make every day more pleasurable is a good starting point, along with accepting who you are and knowing what you can and can't change. We often look to external, material things to make us happy, but this feeling is fleeting and as soon as the initial buzz wears off, we are back to where we started. Experts agree it is much better to look within yourself for true contentment. Check in with yourself daily and take steps to build your self-esteem. Know your true value and give thanks for all the blessings in your world, and happiness will become your natural state of mind.

This section looks at what makes you happy and highlights some of the ways that you can lift your spirits and experience more joy every day.

"MOST FOLKS ARE AS HAPPY AS THEY MAKE UP
THEIR MINDS TO BE."
Abraham Lincoln

What is preventing you
from experiencing true
happiness? Identify the
areas in your life where
you could be happier,
whether it's your career,
your personal life or
something else.

....

....

....

....

....

....

....

....

....

....

....

....

....

....

....

....

....

....

....

For every area you've
identified, think of one
practical thing you could do
to improve your happiness.

Your happy place visualization to
inspire feelings
of contentment

You are sitting in the garden cocooned by flowers; beautiful blooms of every description are gathered in large clumps and bushes. It's a warm sunny day, and you feel totally at peace. Bathed in the bright sunshine, you let your body relax. The birds are tweeting, chirruping in the trees above your head. You can hear the leaves and branches rustle, and you know they're there, watching and accepting you into their world. Butterflies dance before your eyes, they flit from leaf to flower in a carnival of colour and pattern, and you marvel at the artistry of nature.

Ahead you see the purple haze of lavender and smell its sweet scent mixed with the roses as it drifts upon the breeze and enlivens your senses. You can almost taste it. The garden is at its peak. Every element works together and complements each other. It feels like the world is in perfect harmony. You smile. What could be better than sitting here, enjoying the wonder of nature?

You breathe in this contentment.

Drink in the sweetness and let happiness wash over you.

"I CHOOSE HAPPINESS EVERY DAY"

....

....

....

....

Consider how easy it was
to let yourself relax into   ....
the visualization. What was
your favourite part?   ....

....

....

....

....

....

....

....   List the parts of your own
garden that make you
....   happy. Or, if you don't have
a garden, think about the
....   favourite parts of
your local park.

....

....

....

....

"THE ART OF BEING HAPPY LIES IN THE POWER OF
EXTRACTING HAPPINESS FROM COMMON THINGS."
Henry Ward Beecher

The beautiful sound of bird song is one of nature's gifts. The lilting
harmonies, as the feathered orchestra of the sky come together to
perform, is enough to lift the spirits and put a spring in anyone's
step. It's a sound we associate with the warmer seasons, with those
first shoots bursting through the soil, and the long sunnier days.

The next time you hear the birds sing, whether you're
outside, by a window or simply playing a playlist of bird
sounds, try to identify the different voices. Focus on the trail
of each sound. Notice how the strands of melody are all unique
but come together to create something special. Close your eyes
and enjoy the moment.

What sounds do you enjoy in nature?
Make a list of the sounds that make you smile every
time you hear them.

....

....

....

Think of a time when you felt really happy. Are there
any sounds that you associate with this moment? If
so, what are they?

....

....

....

> "BE HAPPY FOR THIS MOMENT. THIS MOMENT
> IS YOUR LIFE."
> Omar Khayyam

The sweet and mellow scent of lavender is something we associate with a garden in bloom. This wonderfully calming herb has been around for thousands of years. In ancient Rome and Greece it was a popular addition to bath water as it was thought to purify body and soul, and the Egyptians used it in the mummification process. Today it's renowned for its soothing properties.

The gentle aroma calms the mind and promotes harmony, making it the perfect choice for those who want to feel happy. To enhance the visualization massage into pulse points and inhale.

Let your mind wander and think of those moments when you experienced joy. What could you smell, or what scents remind you of that moment?

....

....

....

....

List all the scents that make you feel happy, for example, your favourite meal, your mum's perfume...

....

....

....

....

Have you ever stood barefoot on a carpet of grass, either in your garden or at the park? The sensation of the tiny blades beneath the soles of your feet is invigorating. The coolness you feel as you press into the fresh green shoots, is instantly uplifting. Even if you don't fancy walking barefoot, simply smoothing the palm of your hand over a patch of lawn is enough to make you smile.

Try it. Replay the experience in your mind and use it to enhance the visualization. Let the sensation of touch remind you that there is joy in the small things.

What textures and materials do like the feel of? Perhaps you're a fan of velvet or satin, or you prefer the rough feel of wood, or the icy kiss of the snow.

....
....
....
....
....
....
....

....
....
....
....
....
....
....
....

List five things that instantly make you happy when you touch them. Perhaps it's the feeling of a soft jumper against your skin or the texture of a round, smooth pebble.

Get into the habit of finding happiness in every moment, with a simple mindful technique that encourages you to stay present and engage with your environment. Connecting in this way will help you feel calm and content. You will also start to see the good things that are all around you.

Stand outside, in your garden, on the street, in a local park, the location is up to you. Just set aside half an hour to really appreciate your surroundings.

1. Find a spot where you feel comfortable and let your gaze rest on one thing that stands out to you. This could be anything – a flower, a lamppost, a leaf, whatever has caught your attention in that moment.

2. Spend a few minutes studying this object, taking in every aspect from its size, shape, colour, and any unusual markings. If your mind begins to wander, bring it back to the object. See and appreciate the beauty of the object you've chosen.

3. When you're ready, turn your attention to what you can smell. Are there any interesting aroma's that stand out? What do they remind you of?

4. Now consider what you can taste. Take a gulp of air and let it settle on your tongue. Is it fresh, bitter, sweet?

5. Next think about all the sounds that surround you. Pick one that stands out and home in on it. Focus all your attention on this noise.

6. Finally, take a moment to be grateful for all the things you can see, smell, taste and hear. Find happiness in the wonder of everything around you.

How did you find the exercise? What did you enjoy
most about the experience and how did it
make you feel?

....

....

....

....

....

....

....

....

Bring to mind the object you picked and take a few
minutes to describe it.

....

....

....

....

....

....

....

....

When you are present and engage your senses,
everything becomes vivid, full of colour, life and joy.
You can relive the joyful emotions you experienced,
just by recalling those moments.

your affirmation for happiness

"I USE MY SENSES TO FULLY APPRECIATE AND
EXPERIENCE JOY"

Use this space to record how you plan on achieving a
sense of happiness in the future.

....

....

....

....

....

....

....

....

....

....

....

....

....

....

....

....

....

....

Love

Love is the fundamental source of life. It is where it all begins. All encompassing but never demanding, it is a complex emotion, from the gentle nurturing love of a mother for her child to that first rush of passion between lovers. Love is many things. It cannot be pigeonholed, only accepted with grace and understanding. It is the quest of the lonely and the curse of the broken-hearted. An object of study for artists and poets, and the subject of so many songs – love is an eternal journey, and it starts with you.

Learning to love and appreciate yourself is the key to everything. Accepting who you are and embracing your unique nature are the first steps. When you truly love and respect yourself, your heart opens like a flower, and you're able to give and receive love, to share it in new ways. Never judgemental and always encouraging, love is a healing balm that has the power to unite people around the world. It builds bridges and melts hearts, and can help you see and experience the wonder in every day.

This section helps you open your heart and make loving connections, starting with the most important connection of all: the relationship you have with yourself.

"LIFE IS THE FLOWER FOR WHICH LOVE IS THE HONEY."
Victor Hugo

How loved do you feel,
right now? Think about
your relationship with your
family, friends and anyone
else in your life.

....

....

....

....

....

....

....

....

....

List the people that make
you feel loved. In what
ways do they show their
love for you?

What is holding you
back from experiencing
more love? Identify your
'love' blocks. For example,
does low self-esteem make
you feel as though you don't
deserve love?

....

....

....

....

....

....

Your happy place visualization to
help you open your heart to love

You are sitting on a park bench, taking in the view. Trees line the path, tall and billowing, their wide leaves flutter in the breeze. A gust of wind claws at your face and you pull your coat tighter around you. Up ahead, an elderly couple walk arm in arm, oblivious to the cold. The woman nestles into the man's shoulder and for a moment their eyes lock as a smile settles upon her lips. He brushes a strand of hair from her cheek, and whispers something that makes her chuckle. Then they move on, step-by-step, in perfect sequence.

You smile as you watch them go. You can sense the bond between them and the memories they hold dear. The love that flows from them wraps around you; it's a warmth that spreads from deep within your chest and infiltrates every part of your being. You feel light as a feather, on top of the world but also a part of it.

And in this moment you realise just how much love binds us together. A connection between family, friends, lovers and strangers. And it starts with loving yourself.

"I AM FILLED WITH LIGHT AND LOVE"

How did this visualization
make you feel about the
power of love in your life?

....
....
....
....
....
....
....
....
....
....

....
....
....
....
....
....
....
....
....
....

How easy did you find it to
feel the binding qualities
of love by the end of the
visualization?

"TO LOVE ONESELF IS THE BEGINNING OF
A LIFELONG ROMANCE."
Oscar Wilde

Sweet nothings are those words of comfort, those compliments that strike at the heart of who we are and tell us that we're special. Music to the ears, they're the accompaniment of love and a way to express how we feel. Just as the couple in the visualization shared whispered words of love, so you can experience this too, with or without a partner.

Make a list of all the things you love about yourself –
this can include qualities, talents and gifts, or simple
things like your smile. If you struggle with this, ask a
good friend or family member to help.

....

....

....

....

....

....

....

....

....

....

....

Once you've compiled the list, use it as inspiration for a
different loving affirmation each day. Tell yourself why you are
brilliant and believe it!

"LET US ALWAYS MEET EACH OTHER WITH A SMILE,
FOR THE SMILE IS THE BEGINNING OF LOVE."
Mother Teresa

Smells have the power to transport us back in time. The whiff of a scent from childhood conjures feelings of love and acceptance. We feel instantly connected to that moment and the emotion we felt. The scent of love is different for everyone. For some it's a certain perfume or product, for others it's the sweet aroma of a rose in bloom, or the smell of someone special.

Transport yourself back to a time when you felt truly loved. What can you smell? Even if there isn't a scent that you associate with this emotion, think about the smells that you love and make you feel special and list them below.

....

....

....

....

....

....

....

....

....

....

....

If you have a favourite perfume, body oil or a bath soak, use it often. Treat yourself because you deserve it. Self-love is about being kind to yourself, so start with the little things that make you smile.

Touch is an important way to show others you care, from the brief touch of a hand on the shoulder to a massive bear hug. Touch is the language of love, and something we all crave. Some people are more comfortable with it than others, like the couple in the visualization walking arm in arm, connected by the simplest touch. Whether you're shaking hands or wiping away someone's tears, there's a closeness, an intimacy that comes with touching. To do it, you must open your heart and reach out.

How you do you feel about hugs? Do you give them freely or shy away?

Who gives your favourite hugs? What makes them so good?

Make a list of the people in your life that you like to hug and make a point of hugging them more!

Practise self-love with a self-hug. Wrap your arms around your body and gently rub your shoulders with your hands. Imagine you're hugging someone you care about and feel the love.

When we love ourselves, we are actually saying "you deserve to be loved". This is a powerful message to the subconscious mind, which affects how we think, feel and react to others. It means we are more likely to act in a loving way with those we meet and interact with.

To help you build a strong and loving
core from which you can let the love
flow, practise this exercise daily.

1. Stand in front of a full-length mirror. Gaze at your reflection and embrace the person that you are. Instead of focusing on any imperfections, look at your entire reflection and recognize that you are this amazing person who has the power to impact upon the lives of others.

2. Look into your eyes and see the beauty of your soul shine through.

3. Smile, even if you don't feel like smiling. Go through the motions and look at how this one expression lights up your face. See the smile reach your eyes and notice how they come alive.

4. Draw your attention to the middle of your chest. This is where your heart chakra is located. This energy centre is associated with love, and can help you heal and also feel and share this emotion.

5. Picture a spinning ball of pink light in the centre of your chest. See it getting bigger and brighter, sending waves of loving energy outward to the world.

6. To finish, say "I love and accept myself. I am beautiful in every way."

How did you feel during
the exercise? Did you find
it easy to see your
inner beauty?

....

....

....

....

....

....

....

....

....

....

....

....

....

....

Identify three ways you
could be more loving to
yourself. For example, do
you need to be more patient
with yourself?

....

....

....

....

....

....

Identify three ways you
could be more loving with
others, whether it's telling
your friends and family
how much you love them or
simply complimenting
a colleague.

....

....

your affirmation for love

"I LET LOVE FLOW IN MY LIFE"

Use this space to record how you plan on practising love in the future.

....

....

....

....

....

....

....

....

....

....

....

....

....

....

....

....

....

....

Depression

Globally, its estimated that over 264 million people suffer with depression, making it one of the leading causes of disability and illness in the world today. While we all go through short periods when we feel low and not ourselves, we're generally able to move on from them, with a little self-care and support. Clinical depression is not the same. It's a very real illness, which has a huge impact on everything, from personal relationships to work, life and education.

Symptoms

Sufferers report feeling sad for long periods of time. They struggle with feelings of hopelessness and despair, and become unable to cope with normal life. Everyday things that they once enjoyed no longer interest them, and even simple things like getting out of bed become a huge effort. In general, people with depression will often retreat from the world and those who care about them, in a bid to disconnect completely. The worst-case scenario is that they take their own lives – around 800,000 people commit suicide every year and it's the second leading cause of death in 15–29-year-olds. There are physical symptoms too, with the majority of sufferers reporting aches and pains, general fatigue and loss of libido.

The triggers

According to research, women tend to suffer with depression more than men, and children can also be diagnosed with it. In fact one in 10 people will experience some form of depression during their lifetime. While the causes are different for everyone, common triggers include life-changing events like bereavement or redundancy, suffering abuse, hormonal changes and a stressful lifestyle. For men, toxic masculinity – such as the fear of expressing emotions or opening up to someone – can make depression worse.

The way forward

Treatment for depression varies depending on the type of depression and the severity. Diet, exercise and lifestyle changes can help, along with counselling and behavioural therapy. Antidepressants may also be prescribed in some cases. A self-care routine is key when tackling depression, and taking time out to calm the mind, using meditation and mindfulness techniques can be beneficial and help sufferers feel more positive in their outlook.

Inspiration

Inspiration can bring you to life in a matter of moments. It is a spark, an idea, an emotion that pushes you out of your comfort zone. It is a flash of light that illuminates the mind and forces you into creative action, and it speaks to you through each of your senses.

To the ancients it was almost supernatural and belonged to the realm of the gods and other spiritual beings like the Greek muses. They could be called upon for inspiration and petitioned with offerings and prayers. Today, we know that it is something that happens within us, and that it can be caused by almost anything: a chance word, a picture, a beautiful piece of music...

Whatever is the catalyst the result is always the same. When you feel inspired, there's a sense of urgency to do something that you haven't done before, to go beyond and create. The imagination is fired and you are ready, hopeful, daring to dream and dreaming to dare.

This section helps you see and recognize the inspiration in your world. It shows you how to tap into this creative well and ignite the spark of your imagination.

"INSPIRATION IS AN AWAKENING, A QUICKENING OF
ALL MAN'S FACULTIES, AND IT IS MANIFESTED IN ALL
HIGH ARTISTIC ACHIEVEMENTS."
Giacomo Puccini

Identify what inspires you
in your everyday life. List
at least three things.

....

....

....

....

....

....

....

....

....

....

....

....

....

When do you feel at your
most creative? When
you first wake up?
During a walk?

....

....

....

When do you feel at your
least creative? Think about
why this might be.

....

....

....

....

Your happy place visualization to
help you find inspiration

Take a deep breath in and smell the fresh scent of the pine forest. Everywhere you turn there are trees like tall spears shooting upward. It is cool in here. The dampness is soothing, and you feel relaxed and refreshed. The earth is springy underfoot, as if the ground is cushioning your every move. The colours of nature seep under your skin, from the deep emerald green of needle-thin leaves to the muddy brown dirt of the forest floor.

Rivers of sunlight stream through the trees, casting spotlights among the greenery. They illuminate the forest and bring new growth. Wherever you turn you see movement, colour and life. The trees and the leaves are glistening.

You spin around, and for every turn more light and colour explode from your fingertips.

This is a place of inspiration. A place where you can feel potential and the promise of renewal.

You draw a deep breath in and feel a light go on in your mind as your imagination awakens.

You exhale and let the creativity flow.

"MY CREATIVITY GROWS AS MY SENSES AWAKEN"

....

....

....

....

What part of the   ....
visualization made you feel
the most inspired?   ....

....

....

....

....

....

....

....

....

....   **Are there any similar**
                                        settings nearby that inspire
....   **you? Which of them stand**
                                        out and why?
....

....

....

....

> "CREATIVITY IS CONTAGIOUS, PASS IT ON."
> Albert Einstein

The whooshing sound of the wind as it blows through the trees is exhilarating; it's an energizing force of nature. Just like the creative energy that flows through every one of us, it sweeps through your life and takes over in an instant. Inspiration is like this, there's an initial rush of excitement, a gust that comes from out of nowhere and takes you on a ride. Imagine you are a leaf upon the wind of inspiration. Where will it take you?

Let yourself daydream and give your thoughts the freedom to wander. When you've finished, write down what you can remember: words, images and ideas.

....

....

....

....

....

....

....

....

....

....

....

....

"IN ALL THINGS OF NATURE THERE IS SOMETHING
MARVELLOUS."
Aristotle

The crisp, woody scent of pine oil has an invigorating effect on body and mind. It promotes energy, stimulates the senses and helps you feel alert and creative. Derived from the pine tree, which was praised in folklore for the way it would grow and reach for the sun's rays, this essential oil has the power to transport you to the heart of the forest.

Use 5–6 drops in an oil burner or add to a small bowl of warm water and inhale the scented steam. Close your eyes and picture yourself standing among the sea of pine trees in the visualization. Set your imagination free and let the aromatic aroma inspire you.

If you feel inspired, put pen to paper and write anything that comes to mind.

....

....

....

....

....

....

....

....

....

....

The sense of touch can reveal so much more than we might think, whether it's the feeling of the bark on a tree or the smooth glossiness of a leaf. When you take away the other senses and leave touch, you begin to look at things intuitively. You become more creative and engage your imagination, relying solely on what you can feel. Your mind conjures up images, and this is a great starting point for new ideas, inspiration and change.

Set yourself a challenge to look at an object in a new way, by relying only on your sense of touch, and then journal what you feel and see intuitively.

Pick something that you are familiar with, like a shell or crystal. Close your eyes and explore the object with your fingers. Let your mind wander, and let the object inspire you.

Write a few words or a poem in response to this exercise.

....

....

....

....

....

....

....

....

....

....

....

Nature has been a source of inspiration for poets, writers, artists and entrepreneurs throughout history. Immersing yourself in the natural world and fully engaging with your surroundings is liberating. It lifts the spirits, boosts levels of the feel-good hormone serotonin and provides plenty of stimulus for the mind. The landscape is inspiring, particularly in the countryside, and you don't have to go on a long ramble to gain the benefits. A gentle walk can provide a spark of creativity, which will carry you through the day.

Make sure you're prepared before you go on your walk. Dress accordingly and with the appropriate footwear for the landscape. Take a notepad and pen to capture any moments of inspiration.

1. Breathe in your surroundings as you walk. Imagine drawing a breath from deep in your belly and taking in as much oxygen as you can. As you breathe out, relax your body and let any tension fall away.

2. Engage all your senses during your stroll. Take note of what you can see, look at the shapes and colours of nature. What do they remind you of? Think about the smells, the scent of the flowers, the fresh sweet air and how it tastes. Then turn your attention to what you can hear. Listen to the sounds of your own footsteps and your breathing. Try to identify the different sounds that you hear during your journey.

3. Throughout your walk, take note of your feelings. If something captures your attention, ask yourself why, then consider how it made you feel.

4. Don't rush, give yourself plenty of time to experience everything and if you feel the need to stop and drink everything in, do it.

5. Allow yourself the time to be inspired.

Use this space to reflect
upon your walk. What
did you enjoy about the
experience? What, if
anything, did you dislike?

....

....

....

....

....

....

....

....

....

....

....

....

....

List everything you saw
that had an impact
upon you.

....

....

....

....

Write a couple of sentences
or a poem in response
to your walk.

....

....

....

....

....

your affirmation for **inspiration**

"I TAKE INSPIRATION FROM MY SURROUNDINGS"

Use this space to record how you plan on achieving a
sense of inspiration in the future.

....

....

....

....

....

....

....

....

....

....

....

....

....

....

....

....

....

....

....

....

Motivation

Motivation is the driving force that pushes us forward to achieve our dreams. It's the impetus to strike and the urge to keep going, even when the going gets tough. When we're motivated, we are in the zone, going with the flow of life and making things happen. It's a wonderful uplifting feeling that sweeps through our world and promotes a sense of purpose, but it isn't always a given.

Motivation can ebb and flow throughout our life, and we have to work at keeping it constant. Periods of stress can play havoc with our willpower. This, along with setbacks and unexpected challenges, can faze us and send any motivation we had running for the hills. It's at these moments that we need to dig deep and find the drive not only to keep going, but to keep going with urgency and enthusiasm. Once we start the journey toward motivation, it becomes a natural process, and we build momentum quickly.

This section aims to boost your motivation – showing you how to find it, maintain it and use it as an empowering force in your life.

"IF YOU FELL DOWN YESTERDAY, STAND UP TODAY."
H. G. Wells

When do you feel at your
most motivated? During
the day? After meeting
with friends?

....

....

....

....

....

....

....

....

....

....

....

....

....

....

When do you feel the least
motivated? After a long
day? When your plans
get cancelled?

Identify your blocks to
motivation, for example,
if something doesn't go to
plan, does it knock your
confidence and make you
lose your motivation?

....

....

....

....

....

....

Your happy place visualization to
help you feel motivated

You gaze up at powdery blue skies. Your sun hat flops across your brow, shielding you from the brightness, and you close your eyes. It's then that you notice the humming, a low vibration that draws you in. The deep thrum resonates within, and you recognize it for what it is: worker bees on a mission. The buzzing picks up speed and intensity. It's as if there's a chorus serenading you, encouraging you to join in and unleash your own unique song.

You open your eyes and see the object of their attention, the beautiful flowering bush seems to shimmer with a flurry of wings as they hop from each flower head. You marvel at their industry, at the passion and energy with which they work. It sparks a need in you to apply your own mind, to do something of value and purpose.

Your thoughts are whirling as the bee song reaches its crescendo. You take a breath and feel your motivation growing.

It's time to get moving, to get started and unleash your passion upon the world. Just like the bees, you are bristling with energy and enthusiasm. You can feel it buzzing beneath your skin.

There is no stopping you now!

"WITH EACH BREATH I AM ENERGISED AND MOTIVATED"

How did the visualization make you feel? Could you sense your energy growing with the buzz of the bees?

....
....
....
....
....
....
....
....
....
....

....
....
....
....
....
....
....
....
....

Think of the bees and how they work together as a team for a common purpose. Think of a time when you worked in a team to achieve a goal. What did you learn from that experience? Identify three traits that helped you find success.

> "THE SECRET OF GETTING AHEAD IS
> GETTING STARTED."
> Mark Twain

The sound of bees buzzing is invigorating. The noise occurs when the bees' wings vibrate together, and the larger the bee, the deeper the hum. It's also a form of communication and a way to let some flowers know that bees are present. In response, they make their nectar sweeter and more available. As such, the buzz is a "tool" that helps the bees shake the nectar from the flower head and motivates the flower into action too.

What kind of noise motivates you? Perhaps you have a favourite song or playlist, or a type of instrument that gets you moving. Make a list of the sounds that spur you into action.

....

....

....

....

Now think about words and phrases that might motivate you. Even if you can't think of any, do some digging and find a couple of phrases that inspire you and write them below.

....

....

....

....

"IF YOU CAN DREAM IT, YOU CAN DO IT."
Walt Disney

Fragrant flowers will always attract the bees first, which is not surprising when you consider it's the sugary nectar they want, but while sweet-scented blooms might get our pollinators going, it's a different story when it comes to the human brain. Research shows that different aromas have the power to motivate us.

One of the best smells to fire up the brain is the aroma of coffee brewing. Even if you're not a fan of the dark stuff, the scent alone can make a difference to mental agility and activity.

Conduct an experiment and brew a cup of coffee.
Spend five minutes inhaling the heady aroma. Draw
it in through the nose and out through the mouth.
Then write a few sentences to describe how you feel.

....

....

....

....

Now think about the smells that get you moving.
Make a list of invigorating scents and think of ways
that you can introduce them into your world.

....

....

....

....

Smooth, thick and deliciously sweet, honey is a delight to eat, but even if you're not a fan of the taste, you can still experience the benefits of the bees bounty by applying it to your skin. Honey is a natural moisturiser, it's packed full of antioxidants and enzymes, and can be used to nourish and plump, as well as helping to remove excess oil.

Pamper yourself and get energized for the day ahead, by applying a thin layer of honey to your body and face after your morning shower. Enjoy the soothing sensation for a couple of minutes, then rinse off with warm water.

How does your skin look and feel? How did the honey treatment make you feel inside: relaxed, motivated, energized?

....

....

....

....

....

....

....

....

....

....

....

Five minutes of self-care and pampering in the morning, can put you in the right frame of mind, to step out, with confidence and motivation.

One of the best ways to boost self-motivation is to recognize what you have achieved so far and why it worked for you. We can be our own worst critics, berating ourselves for past mistakes and focusing on the negative, which completely destroys motivation and leaves us feeling deflated. Instead, make a point of recognizing what you have done well, celebrate your victories, however small, and develop a gratitude attitude with the following exercise.

This exercise should be carried out in two parts: the first in the morning before you start your day, and the second in the evening before bed. You'll need a keepsake box and lots of small pieces of paper.

1. In the morning, write down three things that you're grateful for. These could be big things like your health, home, family, friends, or smaller things, like your morning cuppa. Make sure you write each blessing on a separate piece of paper. In the evening, think back on your day and think of three things that went well for you. Write a couple of sentences for each thing, on three separate pieces of paper, and add them to the box.

2. Over the course of the week, repeat the exercise morning and night. At the end of the week, dip your hand into the box and pull out three pieces of paper. Read them and recap on what you have achieved so far, and just how wonderful your life is.

3. Whenever you're in need of motivation, turn to your keepsake box. You should find plenty of inspiration in there to put you in a positive mindset.

Think about the gratitude exercise. How easy did you
find it to pick out successes and blessings?
If you found it difficult, consider why. Do you
struggle to see the positive, or perhaps you're
unnecessarily hard on yourself?

....

....

....

....

....

....

....

....

Make a list of ways that you can adopt a positive
attitude every day. Things like silencing your
internal critic or switching up your thoughts and
focusing on the best outcome instead of the worst.

....

....

....

....

....

....

....

....

your affirmation for motivation

"EVERY SUCCESS, BIG OR SMALL, MOTIVATES ME TO ACHIEVE MORE"

Use this space to record how you plan on achieving a sense of motivation in the future.

....

....

....

....

....

....

....

....

....

....

....

....

....

....

....

....

....

Rejuvenation

Life is a series of ups and downs, and like any journey there are times when we need to rest, regroup and recharge our batteries. The weight of the world wears heavy on tired shoulders and at our lowest ebb we need extra impetus to rise up, renewed and ready for the next stage. It is then that we need rejuvenation the most, to feel the fervour, and jump back in with even more enthusiasm.

Rejuvenation is not just about bouncing back, it's about re-animating body, mind and spirit, and in some cases, completely, reinventing yourself. It's that feeling of firing up your core energy and facing each day with fresh hope. Potential is at the heart of rejuvenation. Every moment is filled with opportunities to start again and manifest the life you want. When you're rejuvenated, you feel enlivened, empowered and raring to go. The oomph that was lost returns threefold and there's a sense that nothing can stop you.

This section looks at the power of rejuvenation and how you can embrace this for yourself.

> "WE MUST ALWAYS CHANGE, RENEW, REJUVENATE
> OURSELVES; OTHERWISE, WE HARDEN."
> Johann Wolfgang von Goethe

What things do you do to lift your spirits? Make a list of your 'go-to' energy boosters. For example, chatting to a loved one or going for a run.

....

....

....

....

....

....

....

....

....

....

....

....

What activities leave you feeling energized and excited? How often are you able to make time for them?

Look at the two lists you've compiled and think of a way of incorporating suggestions from both to rejuvenate your weekly schedule.

....

....

....

....

....

....

....

Your happy place visualization
to help you feel rejuvenated

You are standing on a mountain top, your feet cushioned by damp, mossy grass. The view stretches out before you, undulating waves of valley that sprawl as far as the eye can see. The shadowy horizon cradles the sun, sending tendrils of light into the sky and there's a sense of anticipation, of a day about to begin. The wind whips at your heels, it nudges you closer to the edge, but you do not feel afraid. You are exhilarated.

You draw in a lungful of air. It feels fresh, vibrant, full of opportunity. Your cheeks flush with colour as the breeze grazes your face. The wind seems to blow through you, stealing away your worries and fears. You open your arms wide, let the air wrap around you. If you closed your eyes and made a wish you would lift from the mountain top, like a leaf caught in flight.

You breathe in and hold on to this feeling of weightlessness. You can feel excitement bristling beneath your skin. You step forward and let the air support you. This is your time to soar!

"EVERY CELL IN MY BODY IS REJUVENATED AND IMBUED WITH VIBRANT LIGHT"

Did you find it easy to
picture yourself standing
on a mountain top?
How did it feel so close
to the edge?

....

....

....

....

....

....

....

....

....

....

....

....

....

Which other locations
and settings in nature
make you feel positive and
energized? Make a list of
your favourites.

Even if you can't visit some
of the places on your list,
think of ways that you can
incorporate them into your
home, in pictures, prints,
patterns and textures, and
write down your ideas.

....

....

....

....

....

....

....

"LIFE SEEMS TO GO ON WITHOUT EFFORT WHEN I AM FILLED WITH MUSIC."
George Eliot

Music has the ability to lift the spirits and transport you to another world. Its revitalising power lies in toe-tapping tunes and upbeat melodies that encourage movement. This in turn boosts feel-good hormones. Some tracks remind us of times when we felt at our brightest and best, but we don't have to wait for the music and the memory to feel right. We can create sound triggers that we can call on when we need rejuvenation.

Identify three songs/pieces of music that instantly lift your spirits and give you a feeling of renewed hope.

....

....

Play each one, and as you do, sing or dance along. Throw yourself into the spirit of the music and imagine you're under the spotlight.

For each song, write a word that sums up how you feel when you hear it. You might notice that one in particular stands out. If so, focus on this song and make it your rejuvenation theme tune.

....

....

Replay the tune in your mind and each time focus on how it feels when you hear the song. Soon it will become natural for you to feel rejuvenated when you replay a snippet of the song in your mind.

"RELAX. REFRESH. RENEW. PLAY. SING. LAUGH. ENJOY.
FORGIVE. DANCE. LOVE. HUG. SHARE. KISS. CREATE.
EXPLORE. HOPE. LISTEN. DARE. TRUST. DREAM. LEARN."
Steve Maraboli

What does rejuvenation smell like? It is different for everyone, but experts suggest the fresher the scent, the more uplifting the effect. Fruity citrus smells are instantly invigorating, which is why they're used in cleaning products. Minty aromas will also put a pep in your step as they're astringent and stimulate the mind and nervous system, while aromatic, herby smells also have their place when it comes revitalizing body and spirit – think tea tree, parsley, and rosemary.

Make a list of herbal and citrus scents. Include your favourites, and also opt for ones that you don't know that well.

....

....

....

Over the next few weeks, go through the list one by one and seek out each scent. Close your eyes and inhale the aroma. Think of a few words to describe how the scent made you feel.

....

....

....

When you're done, you should be able to identify at least one scent that makes you feel revitalized.

Massage is a practice based on touch, which stimulates the lymphatic system. This in turn helps the body eliminate toxins that have built up, causing you to feel sluggish and unwell. It alleviates stress and can also help you relax, so it works on many levels, depending on the type of massage you have. Self-message is something we can all do to benefit our health and wellbeing and give ourselves a much-needed boost.

You don't need to invest in any special oil your usual body lotion works just as well. Follow your body, and work with what feels good to you. Start with your feet and massage the oil into each sole. Use your thumb and fingers to work it in, kneading and using circular patterns. Cover the base, sides and top of each foot. From here you can go on to massage your ankles and calves, or your hands.

How did the massage feel? You might want to use this space to record what you did to help you create a self-massage plan for the future.

....

....

....

....

....

....

....

....

....

....

....

Crystal therapy is a healing practice that is effective, when it comes to recharging body and mind. Crystals can be used to amplify and reflect energy, and you don't have to be an expert to glean the benefits. Simply holding the crystal of your choice for a few minutes is enough to see results, but you can take this a step further by combining the power of breathing and positive thought.

This exercise, when practised regularly, will help you feel rejuvenated. You'll need a piece of quartz crystal.

1. Find a comfortable place to sit and cup the crystal in the palms of your hands.
2. Close your eyes and turn your attention to your breath. Take a deep breath in and imagine that you're drawing it through the soles of your feet, up into your lungs.
3. As you release the breath, imagine releasing it over the top of your head, down your spine and out through your feet back into the earth.
4. Continue to breathe in this loop for a couple of minutes or until your mind has cleared.
5. Now as you inhale, imagine you are drawing energy from the crystal. It passes like a stream of light into both hands, along your arms and through your entire body.
6. Continue to breathe the energy in for a couple of minutes, then as you exhale say "I am revitalized" in your head.
7. Carry on breathing in, drawing breath from the earth and energy from the crystal, and then repeat the positive affirmation as you exhale for another minute.
8. When you're finished stand up and give your entire body a shake, then relax and let the energy settle.

Start by thinking about
how you felt before you
started the exercise.
Describe this using three
different words, so you
might say "tired",
"bored", "flat".

....

....

....

....

....

....

....

....

....

....

....

....

....

Now think about the quartz
crystal, how did you feel
when you first held it?
Describe any sensations,
thoughts or feelings
that you had.

....

....

Now think of three words
to sum up how you felt
when you'd finished
the exercise.

....

....

....

....

....

If you enjoyed working with the crystal, do some research into
the properties of different stones, and make a list of the ones
that you'd like to work with.

your affirmation for rejuvenation

"I AM REVITALIZED BY THE THINGS AND PEOPLE
THAT BRING ME JOY"

Use this space to record how you plan on achieving a
sense of rejuvenation in the future.

....

....

....

....

....

....

....

....

....

....

....

....

....

....

....

....

....

....

....

....

Anxiety

Anxiety is more than just feeling worried from time to time. It is defined as feelings of intense turmoil or distress, which impact upon everyday life. It's a medical condition, which manifests in lots of different ways, from physical symptoms like shaking, breathlessness, headaches and chest pain, to strong feelings of dread, irritability and jitteriness. Sufferers often experience prolonged periods of stress and worry, along with shorter, more intense, episodes of complete panic, known as 'panic attacks'.

The facts

According to the World Health Organization, around 264 million people throughout the world suffer with anxiety disorders, with 4.6 per cent of females and 2.6 per cent of males affected around the globe. Research also shows that anxiety occurs more often in Euro/Anglo cultures, compared to African, Asian, Indian, Latin and Middle Eastern cultures. Evidence suggests that anxiety usually develops before the age of 21, with disorders being most prevalent in the teenage years.

Anxiety disorders

Even if you don't consider yourself a sufferer, you may still experience phobias, which are anxiety disorders, as they cause extreme and irrational fear about certain things and situations. Other types of disorders include General Anxiety Disorder, Panic Disorder, Social Phobia, Post Traumatic Stress Disorder, Obsessive Compulsive Disorder and Separation Anxiety.

Coping mechanisms

If you are struggling with worry that you can't shake or any kind of anxiety disorder, medical professionals recommend looking at your diet and general health, taking regular exercise including yoga and Tai Chi, and using breathing techniques to calm and relax the mind. Some talking therapies can also help you deal with what is happening and change your mindset from one of fear to one of focus and balance. There is also a range of apps available that can help you deal with the wide-ranging symptoms of anxiety.

Comfort

Comfort is many things to many people. It's a sense of security, of being safe in the space you find yourself. It's relaxing too. You know that you can be who you want to be, there are no airs or graces. You are you, and that's enough. Comfort is nurturing. There's a sense of returning to the womb, of being sustained physically and emotionally. All your needs are met, and you are loved. It doesn't matter what is going on in the world outside, when you are wrapped in comfort, you are held in a secure embrace.

Comfort is what you make it. We all have different ideas. For some it's curling up with a good book, for others, it's lazing beneath the sun's rays, while for many it's about who you are with, and that feeling of being loved and protected. The good news is we don't have to look to others to provide us with comfort. We can do it ourselves. All we have to do is identify the things that give us comfort and allow some time to enjoy these simple pleasures.

This section aims to create a sense of comfort in your life. It will help you find the space you need to rest and recharge.

"CURE SOMETIMES, TREAT OFTEN, COMFORT ALWAYS."
Hippocrates

What does "comfort" mean
to you, both mentally
and physically?

....

....

....

....

....

....

....

....

....

....

....

....

....

What gives you comfort?
Identify the things in your
life that help you feel safe,
and loved, then make a list.

....

....

....

What makes you feel
uncomfortable? Consider
why that might be.

....

....

....

....

Your happy place visualization
to help you feel a sense of comfort

Take a deep breath in and as you exhale, picture yourself sitting before an open fire. The flames crackle and leap in every direction, they flicker and twist before your eyes. You can feel the warmth from the glow of the embers caressing your skin. You can smell the scent of the wood burning. As you slow your breathing down, you feel a thick, soft blanket around your shoulders. The weight is comforting and you pull it tighter around you, drawing yourself into the smooth folds. Outside it is dark. The velvety sky is littered with stars, and there's a nip to the air, but it doesn't matter, because you are here. You are safe in this snuggly cocoon.

Let the cosy blanket shield you from the outside world.

Let the fire capture your heart.

Breathe, relax, enjoy.

"I AM COCOONED IN COMFORT."

How quickly were you able
to feel a sense of comfort
using the visualization?
Were you able to relax
and imagine feeling
safe and warm?

....
....
....
....
....
....
....
....
....

....
....
....
....
....
....
....
....
....
....

Can you recall a time you
were in a similar setting?
Write down what helped to
comfort you the most.

The gentle crackle of a roaring fire is soothing. It helps to create a warm atmosphere. Combined with the amber glow, it can help you feel cosy even when it's cold outside. It's a reassuring sound, all is well, the fire is still burning, and you are safe and snug. It's the kind of sound that takes you back to childhood, from snuggling up with your family, to warming your hands in front of a bonfire.

Close your eyes right now and imagine the background noise of an open fire. Can you feel the heat upon your face? What does it remind you of? Describe where it takes you.

....

....

....

....

....

Make a list of sounds from childhood that make you feel safe and nurtured.

....

....

....

....

....

....

"COURAGE AND COMFORT, ALL SHALL YET GO WELL."
William Shakespeare

The things in life that provide comfort usually appeal to our basic needs for love, security and nourishment. This goes for scents too. We often favour smells that remind us of times when we felt safe and happy, when we were truly satisfied. This goes some way to explain why the aroma of your favourite meal can create a sense of comfort.

Imagine cooking your favourite meal. Smell the scent of it wafting in the air. How does this make you feel?

....

....

....

....

Go a step further and make a list of your favourite foodie smells, then set yourself the challenge of including three or four of these foods in your weekly menu. Remember that comfort comes when we meet our basic needs, and eating nutritious meals that we love is an act of self-care.

....

....

....

....

Touch is incredibly comforting. It helps us feel like we matter to someone, and that gives us a sense of belonging. We feel nurtured when we are cocooned in a safe space. Something soft and snuggly that cloaks you in comfort has the ability to take you away from the world for just a few minutes and can make a big difference to your wellbeing.

The heavy warmth of a blanket around the shoulders is all it takes to create this feeling. Once more we are transported back to childhood, to the blankets carefully placed around our sleeping form, and the sense of security that this provided.

Find a blanket or duvet, curl up and draw it around you until you are completely covered. Spend as long as you like in this position and let your mind wander.

Before you begin, write your thoughts below. Then note how your thoughts changed after spending time snuggled up in your blanket.

....

....

....

....

....

....

....

....

....

....

We should be able to seek comfort at any time of the day, but especially before we go to sleep. This is the time when we want to switch off from the day, relax and drift into dream. Unfortunately, most of us will suffer from insomnia at some point in our lives, so it's important to practise good sleep habits and to know a technique that will help you destress.

The following exercise aids relaxation and
promotes comfort before bedtime.

1. Lay on your bed and let your mind and body settle with a few deep breaths. Take your time and fall into a natural rhythm. Slow each breath down by counting out five beats each time you inhale and the same when you exhale.

2. Feel your chest relax and soften. Now focus on your tummy, the area below your naval. Imagine that as you breathe in, you breathe in comfort. You might feel this as a warm and cosy sensation, a wave of calm or even a colour that you absorb like white or pink.

3. Feel the comfort spread throughout your stomach region as you exhale. Continue until your tummy feels completely relaxed, then move on to another body part, like your arm or leg.

4. Take your time and move through your body, taking the comfort up into your chest, shoulders and neck, and then finally breathing the feeling into your head, behind the eyes and your scalp.

5. By the time you are finished you should feel deeply relaxed and safe in the space you have created.

How easy or difficult
did you find the comfort
exercise? Was it easy to
isolate parts of your body,
or did you struggle?

....

....

....

....

....

....

....

How quickly were you
able to fall asleep?

If you could picture
comfort as an image or a
colour, what would it be?
Make a list of comforting
shades, patterns and
images, then think about
how you could incorporate
them into your home
and workspace.

....

....

....

....

....

....

....

your affirmation for comfort

"I INHALE COMFORT, I EXHALE STRESS"

Use this space to record how you plan on achieving a
sense of comfort in the future.

....

....

....

....

....

....

....

....

....

....

....

....

....

....

....

....

....

....

Forgiveness

Forgiveness is something we all need. It has the power to heal ourselves and others, and can lift us up when we most need it. Forgiveness does not judge, it is freely given from the heart. Sometimes it is hard to come by, and sometimes it is equally hard to give. When you've been badly hurt the last thing you feel like doing is forgiving the person who has caused you pain, and if that person happens to be you, it can feel impossible.

While it might be easier to hold on to emotions like anger and guilt, in the long run we are doing more harm than good. Forgiveness is the one thing that can set us free. It is our salvation, and once given, it can liberate the soul. Some might consider the very act of forgiving as weak, but the opposite is true. It takes a strong person to open their heart in this way and to release that which has consumed their thoughts. Once you have taken the first step, you'll feel a renewed sense of hope, and a lightness that will carry you forward and on to even greater things.

This section shows you how to welcome forgiveness into your life and use it as a tool for self-healing.

"TO ERR IS HUMAN; TO FORGIVE, DIVINE."
Alexander Pope

....

....

....

....

What is causing you   ....
anger or pain in your
life right now?   ....

....

....

....

....

....

....

....

....   Identify who you need
to forgive in order
....   to move forward.

....

....

....

....

Your happy place visualisation to
help you forgive

You are standing on a small stone bridge which overlooks a stream. It is hidden in a valley in the countryside, cocooned from the outside world. All is quiet here. It's as if you have slipped into another realm or stepped back in time. The sounds of traffic and people are faraway; here there is only the gentle lilt of trickling water, winding its way to wherever it must go. You are mesmerised by the steady flow, the way the ripples twist and curve their path, smoothing over stones that might once have stood in their way.

In your hands you hold a white rose. It represents all that you need to forgive of yourself and others. You take a deep breath in, and as you let the air escape from your lips, you cast it into the water. You watch silently as the stream carries the rose away. A tender breeze wraps spectral arms around you and you feel a sense of comfort and release.

Forgiveness has set you free.

And like the flower that has been swept away, you feel lighter and brighter in every way.

"FORGIVENESS LIFTS ME UP!"

How did it feel to let
go of the rose in the
visualization?

....

....

....

....

....

....

....

....

....

....

....

....

....

....

....

....

....

....

....

....

Could you imagine doing
this for real? Is there
something you could do,
a ritual you could perform
that would help you release
pain and forgive those
who have hurt you?

"HE THAT CANNOT FORGIVE OTHERS BREAKS THE
BRIDGE OVER WHICH HE MUST PASS HIMSELF; FOR
EVERY MAN HAS NEED TO BE FORGIVEN."
Thomas Fuller

The sound of forgiveness comes in the words we choose and the way we use our voice when we express ourselves. This, along with our body language, helps to convey the message, particularly if that message evokes emotion. When we offer forgiveness, it should come from the heart. Our true intentions come through in the tone we use, and the way we say the words, and this is also true of self-forgiveness.

Think of the type of words you might use when offering forgiveness and have a go at writing a couple of sentences below.

....

....

....

....

Read what you have written in your head a couple of times. How does it feel to reread it? You'll instinctively know if the words you've chosen feel right.

....

....

....

....

Now read the words out loud and imagine that the person is in front of you, or if it's yourself, stand in front of mirror and look into your eyes as you speak.

"FORGIVENESS SAYS YOU ARE GIVEN ANOTHER CHANCE TO MAKE A NEW BEGINNING."
Desmond Tutu

When you find it hard to forgive, you can end up holding on to painful emotions for years. There are some theories that suggest buildings are the same. They also absorb emotions in the form of negative energy, so when two people have an argument, the negativity hangs in the air until forgiveness is found. Many experts in the field of energy believe one of the best ways to combat this is to use scent, and in particular the soothing aroma of rose.

Try it for yourself by burning rose-scented candles or adding a few drops of the essential oil to an oil burner.

How does the smell make you feel?

....

....

....

....

....

....

....

....

What other scents help you feel cleansed of negative energy?

List three ways that you could use these fragrances for self-forgiveness, for example running yourself a healing aromatherapy bath.

....

....

....

....

A touch can speak a thousand words. If you are struggling to vocalize how you feel and express your forgiveness, use the power of touch to reach out. You don't have to do anything you don't want to, and if hugging feels too much, then a simple brush of the arm, a hand on the shoulder or even the act of shaking hands can help. If it's you that is seeking your own forgiveness, why not show a little self-love with a hand or foot massage. When we combine the physical with the emotional, we heal on many levels.

Think of other ways that you can show forgiveness in a simple touch or a physical movement. Even building it in to your everyday routine, for example through exercise like yoga.

Find a yoga move that you can use to help you release guilt and pain, and describe it in steps below, then make a point of practising it every day.

....

....

....

....

....

....

....

....

....

....

....

....

Forgiveness is not just an act of release, it also opens the door to a new beginning. We acknowledge the hurt and accept that which has past in order to move forward, with an open heart. We say, "I forgive you" to release us both from pain and sow the seeds for something new. It's important to mark this as a fresh start and to encourage loving energy to flow, so that all involved can heal.

The following exercise helps foster forgiveness
and promote positive energy for the future.

1. Flowers are a gift and often used to symbolize healing. White blooms in particular are associated with purity and forgiveness. Find a white flower that you like this could be a seedling or a bulb and invest in a pot or planter.

2. Add the required amount of compost to the pot, then shape a small hole for the seedling to rest with your fingers. As you do this, think about what forgiveness means to you and what or who you'd like to forgive. You might want to say a few words in your head or out loud, something simple like "I forgive you; I release the past, I am ready to move forward."

3. Next position the seedling into the space and gently cover with the rest of the soil.

4. Pat this down, then water the plant to help it settle and root. As you do this, imagine you are pouring healing energy into the pot.

5. Every time you tend to the plant and water it, say "I embrace this new beginning with love." Then sit back and watch as the plant grows. Nature is great a healer, and watching something you've planted blossom, will instil you with hope.

How do you feel now that you have completed the
exercise and planted the flower? Do you feel lighter,
as though a weight has been lifted? Reflect upon your
thoughts during the ritual.

....

....

....

....

....

....

....

....

Think of at least five things that you'd like to bring
into your life now that forgiveness has allowed
you to let go of the past, for example more love, or
perhaps you'd like to learn something new or visit
somewhere. Draw up a list below.

....

....

....

....

....

....

....

....

your affirmation for forgiveness

I FORGIVE MYSELF AND OTHERS, AND EMBRACE A BRIGHT NEW FUTURE

Use this space to record how you plan on practising forgiveness in the future.

....

....

....

....

....

....

....

....

....

....

....

....

....

....

....

....

....

....

Grace

Grace is a word that conjures up many meanings. In its purest form it is acceptance of the moment and of what life may bring. It does not challenge or complain. Grace goes with the flow and is thankful for everything – the good, the bad, the unconventional. It is synonymous with poise and elegance. When we think of this word, we often think of ballet dancers twirling across the stage, their feet hardly touching the floor, but there are many kinds of grace in life. When someone has grace there's a fluidity to their movements and their actions too. They live in the moment, and as such, become a part of it.

Grace does not judge or complain. It is a gentle quality that resonates inner strength. If you have good grace, you do not act in haste or react with anger when things don't go your way. Instead you take a step back, smile and look for the lessons that can be learned. There is honour in grace, and the recognition that upholding certain values allows you to see the bigger picture.

This section looks at the value of grace and how you can welcome it into your world. It will help you find those moments of grace in every day.

> "GRACE COMES INTO THE SOUL, AS THE MORNING SUN
> INTO THE WORLD."
> Thomas Adams

What does grace mean to you? Write a few words that sum up its meaning for you.

....
....
....
....
....
....
....
....
....

....
....
....
....
....
....
....
....
....

Where might you need more grace in your life? Perhaps when dealing with a certain person or situation?

Your happy place visualization to

help you find the grace in your life

You are lazing in a rowing boat, oars at your side. Going with the flow as the lake glistens beneath you. Ahead there are voices, the sound of children playing, but you cannot see them. Your attention remains with the gliding patterns of the water. Birds tweet in the distance, a group of ducks drift past. It's as if you're watching a performance, a serene dance, of which you are the only spectator.

There's the gentle ring of a bicycle bell and the sound of wheels flying past upon the footpath. It may be a busy spot, a place for people to share and enjoy, but for you it's something more. It's the heart of magic, where the grace of nature flows easily. You watch as a trail of swans sashay toward the water's edge. Their milk-white necks elegantly arched. For them beauty is effortless. They are magnificent as they are.

You take it all in.

Being here.

Being alive.

Bearing witness to the grace of this moment.

"I FIND GRACE IN EVERY MOMENT"

Think about the
visualization and pick out
elements that you might
associate with the
word grace.

....
....
....
....
....
....
....
....
....

....
....
....
....
....
....
....
....
....

If you could picture a scene
anywhere in the world,
real or imagined, where
you might experience a
moment of grace, where
might this be? Describe
the place and conjure the
image in your mind.

"THE IDEAL MAN BEARS THE ACCIDENTS OF LIFE WITH DIGNITY AND GRACE, MAKING THE BEST OF CIRCUMSTANCES."
Aristotle

The word grace describes how we advance through life, both physically and emotionally. It denotes an ease of movement, a fluidity, which is elegant and composed, as if we're floating upon a lake of tranquillity. Water is often associated with emotions and the flow of fate. You only have to listen to the gentle melody of a stream running downhill to get a sense of what grace truly means.

If you can, seek out free-flowing water in nature, like a stream or lake, and spend some time at the water's edge. Watch the gradual movement and the steady journey that it takes. Listen to it as it flows. The sound of silence, stillness, the barely there trickle of ripples.

Consider how you can adopt a similar grace in the way you approach your own life. Perhaps by introducing meditation into your daily routine, or taking a moment to breathe before reacting to a situation?

Make a list of three sounds that can help to encourage the flow of grace in your world.

....

....

....

....

....

....

....

"LEARN TO... BE WHAT YOU ARE AND LEARN TO RESIGN WITH A GOOD GRACE ALL THAT YOU ARE NOT."
Henri Frederic Amiel

The seasons will always come and go. It doesn't matter what is going on in your world, you cannot stop the eternal dance of nature. It is a gentle progression and a good example of grace at work in the environment. Different scents herald the changes, from the fresh dew-laden grass of spring to the sweet scent of summer flowers in full bloom. Autumn takes on a smoky aroma, while in winter the air is icy sharp.

Consider how the seasons move from one to the other and how you might embrace the flow of change in your life with good grace. Pick one scent from each season and describe why you like it.

Just as you found positives in each of the seasonal changes, you can also find positives in the transitions you make.

Reflect upon the previous year and pick at least one positive thing that happened. Can you think of a scent that reminds you of this moment?

....

....

....

How might you recreate this scent for when you want to feel a sense of grace in your everyday life?

....

....

....

Grace is an ethereal quality; it cannot be pinpointed. It simply hangs magically in the air, but if we could touch it, it would feel like a gentle breeze. A smooth, long breath that we draw from our surroundings. It would dance upon our fingers, brush our skin, and pour soothing energy into our lungs.

The air moves all around you. You can feel it and touch it, but you cannot see it, and yet you know it's there. Draw in a long, deep breath. Imagine you are filling your body with light.

Spend five minutes sensing the air around you, then describe how you feel.

....

....

....

....

....

As you move through your day, engage your sense of touch, then make a note of at least five things that you touched and how each one felt.

....

....

....

....

....

They might have been different in texture, but each one had a gift to offer, just as we might encounter different people and situations that also have something to teach us.

Our mind and body are connected in a subtle way, so if we want to invite more grace into our lives, we should also invite it into our physical movements. Building a strong core, and standing with poise and strength are the perfect foundation for grace to flourish.

The following exercise looks at the power of posture:
how you can stand in stillness, and go with the flow.

1. Stand feet hip-width apart. Roll your shoulders back a few times, then let them rest in a comfortable position. Relax your arms and hands at your side.

2. Imagine an invisible thread that journeys through the centre of your body, up along the spine, and out the top of your head. Now imagine someone tugging lightly upon the thread and feel your spine lengthen. Tuck your chin in slightly and feel your neck muscles extend.

3. Breathe, and continue to visualize the thread running upward, but this time imagine each breath sends a stream of light along the thread, up your neck and out the top of your head.

4. As you inhale, draw in your tummy muscles. Pull them in and back, and feel your core tighten. Hold this position if you can and feel your rib cage expand.

5. As you breathe out, relax and soften your chest. Appreciate this moment of stillness as you stand and breathe. Each movement is fluid and graceful.

your affirmation for grace

I CARRY MYSELF WITH GRACE AND DIGNITY

Low Self-Esteem

We all have "off" days, but a lack of self-esteem goes much further than wavering confidence levels. It's a deep-rooted opinion formed about yourself that shapes the way you interact and deal with all sorts of situations, and it has a huge impact on health and wellbeing. From feeling unloved and unworthy, to questioning your abilities and thinking negatively, it's a stigma that you carry, and it can be hard to shake.

Early years

It is estimated that over 85 per cent of the world's population struggles with low self-esteem, and this figure is growing. Issues often start in the formative years of childhood, but then escalate when puberty hits. With a rise in the use of social media, teens often get drawn into comparing themselves with others – anything from the number of "likes" they get on Facebook to negative comments and online bullying can play a part. Teenage girls in particular, struggle. A recent report by the Prince's Trust and the Education Policy Institute found that one in seven girls feels unhappy with the way they look by the end of primary school, and this rises to one in three by the time they reach 14 years of age.

The triggers

Even those who sale through adolescence with their confidence intact can struggle with low self-esteem at some point in their life. Research suggests that around 90 per cent of all women, want to change something about their physical appearance, with as little as 2 per cent believing they are beautiful all of the time.

Sometimes external events can be a trigger to esteem issues: relationship breakdowns, periods of ill health, and sudden changes in circumstance, like redundancy, are all factors when it comes to how self-assured we feel, and the people we surround ourselves with are also important. If we're in the company of people who lift us up, we'll feel more positive about ourselves, but if we're surrounded by people who constantly criticize the way we look and behave, then we'll start to believe in this negative viewpoint.

What you can do

According to the medical professionals, if you suffer from long-term esteem issues it's important to identify the negative beliefs you have about yourself, and then challenge them. This, along with recognizing what you're good at, being kinder to yourself and building positive relationships, are the building blocks to boosting and maintaining a healthy self-esteem.

Clarity

Clarity is something we all need at various points in our lives. It's about seeing clearly, being able to focus on the here and now, which allows us to expand our thinking and look at things from different perspectives. Clarity can be hard to keep a hold of, particularly when we're constantly on the go. It's easy to lose focus, to become swamped with demands and weighed down with worry, and this can cloud our judgement.

When we think with clarity, we know exactly what we want and how to get it. We connect with our inner truth and everything becomes clear. Clarity is like casting a spotlight upon a situation and seeing all the sharp edges and hidden folds. Instead of feeling bogged down, we feel in control, in the zone and ready to reach our goals.

This section looks at how to find clarity and improve your focus. It highlights the steps that you can take to clear the mind of unnecessary debris and move forward renewed, refreshed and raring to go!

> "WHEN PEOPLE WILL NOT WEED THEIR OWN MINDS,
> THEY ARE APT TO BE OVERRUN BY NETTLES."
> Horace Walpole

What seems to always be
on your mind? Identify all
the things that occupy
your thoughts and list
them here.

....

....

....

....

....

....

....

....

....

....

....

....

....

Consider which things on
the list you don't need to
worry about anymore or
that you can't control, and
put a line through them.

Can you think of one thing
that would bring you clarity
at this time? For example,
taking a long walk to clear
your mind of any clutter.

....

....

....

....

....

....

....

Your happy place visualization to

restore a sense of clarity and vision

Imagine you are in your bedroom. It's early evening, but outside it's unnaturally dark. You press your face against the window, feel the cold glass kiss your cheek. The sky is a soup of grey, thick and swirling. There's a sense of expectancy in the air, like everything could change in a second. Your heart hammers in your chest, and your senses are alive. Despite the gloom, you can see, hear and smell everything.

Suddenly the sky splits in two, a scissor of light cuts through the blackness, then you hear the low, rumbling growl of thunder in the distance. It sounds like a thousand wild horses galloping at speed toward you. Again it comes, a white-hot spear that strikes at the heart of the earth in a flash of brightness, and then the sky instantly lightens, and you can see everything. The darkness is gone, replaced by a landscape that shines. And in that moment your mind clears too. It becomes sharper, brighter, infused with dazzling light.

You are focused, ready to move forward. Clarity is yours.

"I FIND CLARITY IN THE DARKNESS"

List all the things
you enjoyed about the
visualization, and why.

....

....

....

....

....

....

....

....

....

....

....

....

....

....

....

....

....

....

Were there any parts you
struggled to visualize?
Think about why
that might be.

....

....

....

....

....

....

....

"CLOSE YOUR EYES TO SEE CLEARLY. BE STILL AND YOU WILL HEAR THE TRUTH."
Ancient Zen saying

There's no doubt that a clap of thunder is dramatic. It grabs and focuses your awareness and is a clear sign that lightning is afoot. There are many sounds in nature that have this effect from the piercing cry of a gull out at sea to the rolling whoosh of a wave against the shore. Nature commands our attention and can help us improve focus and clarity, simply by honing our listening skills.

Identify sounds in nature that instantly grab your attention and consider why this might be. Is it because they're loud, interesting, or because of what they represent?

....

....

....

....

Take one of the sounds from your list and recreate it in your mind. How easy was it to do this? Did you find it hard to focus?

....

....

....

....

Make a point of taking five minutes every day to listen. Whether you're in a conversation with someone, out and about taking a walk, or at your desk. Stop, listen and pick out the key sounds.

"CLARITY OF MIND MEANS CLARITY OF PASSION,
TOO; THIS IS WHY A GREAT AND CLEAR MIND LOVES
ARDENTLY AND SEES DISTINCTLY WHAT IT LOVES."
Blaise Pascal

Rosemary is the herb of the strong and the astute, according to folklore. It was thought that wherever a bush grew freely, you would find a powerful woman. In ancient Greece scholars often wore a sprig upon their brow to improve memory and focus. Today, it's used in tinctures and teas for mental alertness and clarity, and drinking a cup in the morning can help you stay focused throughout the day.

Take a handful of fresh rosemary and steep in a pot with boiling water for at least five minutes. Strain the liquid into a cup and sweeten with a spoonful of honey. Sip, and focus on the fresh aromatic vapours. Inhale, and let the sharp scent enliven your mind. Concentrate solely on the taste. If your mind wanders, bring it back to the tea.

What did you notice about the smell and taste of the tea? As you drank it, did you find your mind wandering and how easy was it to bring your attention back to the tea?

....

....

....

....

....

....

....

....

Drumming is a technique that you can use to help improve clarity. It works in a similar way to the thunderclaps you brought to life in the visualization. It's a sound that is easy to focus on. It is rhythmic and repetitive, and provides the perfect backdrop to a chaotic mind. By focusing on the regular pattern of the beat, you free up space for thoughts and solutions to rise to the surface.

You don't need to invest in a special drum empty tin pots and pans work just as well. Turn them upside down and hit them with a wooden spoon, or if you prefer listen to a playlist of drumming sounds. Relax and let the rhythmic beat take you on a journey. Tap out the rhythm with your hands and imagine that you're beating away the clutter from your mind.

How did you feel during this exercise? Relieved, energized, focused? Did you enjoy the experience?

....

....

....

....

....

....

....

....

....

....

....

....

....

....

Identify other physical activities that might help you find focus and clarity, and list them here.

Many different techniques and tricks can help restore clarity. Simple things like focused breathing, the sound and physical sensation of clear running water, and exercises to keep your mind alert and active.

The following creative exercise combines all these things to help you find your focus and clear away the debris. It's best performed morning or evening and is a great way to destress.

1. Stand beneath a hot or cold shower and spend a few minutes acclimatizing to the feel of the water on your skin. Notice how it feels when it hits your head and trickles down your face. Pay attention to the temperature too.

2. Close your eyes and draw in a long, deep breath. Hold for a count of four slow beats, then release and count out another four slow beats. As you exhale, imagine you're shedding all the clutter that has collected in your mind and body. Feel it being washed away by the water.

3. Continue this cycle of deep breathing and releasing any stress for a couple of minutes.

4. Now turn your attention to the space behind your eyes. Imagine you're looking at an overcast sky. The more you gaze at this view, the more the sky begins to brighten and clear. The clouds gradually disappear, and the hazy grey turns to a sheet of glistening blue. The sun sends rays of light in every direction and the vista is now a brilliant white.

5. All is clear and bright, and you can see for miles. Hold this image in your mind and continue to breathe deeply, enjoying the sensation as the water cleanses body and mind.

How much more focused do you feel after completing the exercise? In the space below, write a rough outline of your daily routine and identify what times of the day you tend to suffer from a lack of clarity.

....
....
....
....
....
....
....
....
....
....
....
....
....
....
....
....
....

Think of three simple things you could do at different points during the day to help restore clarity: things like breathing exercises, taking a mindful moment, etc.

your affirmation for clarity

WITH EVERY BREATH I TAKE, I CLEAR MY HEAD OF CLUTTER

Use this space to record how you plan on achieving a sense of clarity in the future.

....

....

....

....

....

....

....

....

....

....

....

....

....

....

....

....

....

....

Wisdom

Wisdom is something that comes with time and experience. It's an inner knowing, an intuitive force that we can call upon to steer us through the twists and turns of life. It is something we all have and can build upon if we remain open and willing to learn. Wisdom is a gift, and it shines from the eyes of its keeper. It is often hard won, a silver lining to a series of clouds, but once gained, it cannot be taken away. It is with you for life.

You might think that you have to be clever to attain a level of wisdom, but it's not about ingenuity or the size of your IQ. It's the ability to read situations, to understand subtle levels of communication, and how people think and feel. There's an empathy to wisdom, an ability to put yourself in someone else's shoes and sense what they are feeling. Wisdom does not judge or berate; it is compassionate by nature, and instinctively knows that any pearls delivered must also be earned through experience.

This section invites you to discover your inner well of wisdom and learn how you can build upon this intuitive power.

"EXPERIENCE IS NOT WHAT HAPPENS TO YOU; IT'S
WHAT YOU DO WITH WHAT HAPPENS TO YOU."
Aldous Huxley

....

....

....

....

Think of at least one
experience that you've been
through where you gained
some wisdom.

....

....

....

....

....

....

....

....

....

Consider the highs and
lows and the final
outcome, then identify
what you learned from
this experience.

....

....

....

....

....

....

Your happy place visualization to
help you tap into inner wisdom

Close your eyes and imagine you're sitting inside a cave, a giant crevice built into the mountain side. As the light hits the surface of the rock you see the blend of colours – deep sandy reds that swirl into silvery greys and then melt into charcoal. They merge together to create a striking pattern that could match any work of art. You run your hand across the surface, smoothing the stone beneath your palm. It is cool, rough in parts and polished in others.

The air is thick with the scent of the earth, and you are aware of the mountain growing up around you. There is a timeless presence here, an aura of calm. You wonder how many people have sat in this place and pressed their hands into the stone. The combined knowledge and experience of all those visitors is bound into these walls.

You draw down that knowledge with every breath you take.

Gather the wisdom of thousands of years around you like a cloak.

Be still in the moment, open and ready to learn.

"I HAVE ALL THE ANSWERS I NEED WITHIN"

The visualization encourages you to think about wisdom that has been passed down. In your own life, think about those who have taught you something – your parents, grandparents, family members, friends, tutors, colleagues and so on.

This visualization encourages you to think about wisdom that has been passed down to you from others. Who in your life do you turn to for advice?

....

....

....

....

....

....

....

....

....

....

Make a list of the things you have learned from them.

....

....

....

....

....

....

What qualities and traits do they have that help them to remain self-aware and wise?

"WISDOM BEGINS IN WONDER."
Socrates

The sounds that we surround ourselves with are important. They help us build a picture of the world, understand what is going on around us, and communicate thoughts, messages and ideas. If we want to create a reservoir of knowledge and increase intuition, then it's important to engage the sense of hearing, and really listen.

When you're in conversation with someone, make a point of listening more. Instead of jumping in with your own thoughts and opinions, take a step back. Let them speak and hear each word for what it is. Listen to the tone of their voice and the hidden nuances, and you'll gain a deeper understanding of what is going on.

Use this same approach when you're going about your day. Really listen to the sounds that surround you and make a note of what you hear.

Record your thoughts here, and describe all the things you noticed that you wouldn't normally pick up on.

....

....

....

....

....

....

....

....

"KNOWLEDGE COMES, BUT WISDOM LINGERS."
Alfred Lord Tennyson

Open the pages of a book and inhale the scent of knowledge. Breathe in the wisdom as you pore through the words. Even the oldest tome has a whiff of learning about it, a hint that there are secrets hidden between the pages. You might prefer to do your learning online, but there is something joyous about the physical feel and shape of a book in your hands.

Think of all the books you have read that have taught you something important. Make a list of the ones that have resonated the most with you.

....

....

....

....

....

....

Write down some of your favourite quotes from these books.

....

....

....

....

....

....

The sensation of feeling something isn't strictly the domain of the physical world. We feel emotionally, and also intuitively, and we can use these feelings to glean information about current events and for inner guidance. That prickly hair standing on end sensation we get when we feel afraid or those butterflies in the tummy that we experience before something exciting happens – these are all intuitive clues that connect us to our inner wisdom.

Think of a time when you acted on instinct. Describe what happened.

....
....
....
....
....
....
....

....
....
....
....
....
....

Do you get a certain feeling when something isn't right, like a tightness in your chest or stomach? Identify your intuitive clues.

Test this out, by checking in with yourself throughout the day. Notice how you feel at any given moment, and you'll start to become more aware of your intuition working for you.

We have all the answers we need inside. It might be hard to see that at times, and even harder to know how to find them, but they are in there somewhere. When we engage our senses and our intuition, we make it easier for insights to rise to the surface. Carving out time for quiet reflection is also key.

Combine meditation with visualization, and an exercise to open the third eye chakra, when you need to tap into your inner well of wisdom.

1. Find somewhere comfortable to sit, where you won't be disturbed. Switch off your phone, light a scented candle and spend a few minutes breathing deeply to calm your mind.

2. Close your eyes and focus your attention on the area in the middle of your forehead, known as the third eye chakra. This energy centre is associated with the flow of intuition. Imagine there's a tiny purple flower bud in this space. Each time you exhale, one of the petals begins to open until eventually, after several breaths, it's in full bloom.

3. Feel waves of purple energy emanating from the flower.

4. Now take yourself back to the cave in the happy place visualization. Imagine that you are sitting there, in the heart of mountain, only this time it's not a made-up place, it's the seat of your wisdom. Let any thoughts, words or images come and go.

5. If you have a question or a problem that you need help with, bring it to mind and ask for help. Again, let thoughts pass through your head and look for anything that stands out or "feels" right.

6. When you've finished, bring your attention back to the third eye chakra, and the flower. Picture the petals closing, one by one. To finish, take a few long, deep breaths, then open your eyes.

Make a note of any thoughts or ideas that stood out
during the exercise. Even if they don't
make sense now, they could be key to helping you
in the future.

....

....

....

....

....

....

....

....

....

Did you notice anything different about the cave
from the visualization this time around? Did it look
and feel the same, or has something changed?

....

....

....

....

....

....

....

....

....

your affirmation for **wisdom**

"MY INNER SELF GUIDES, PROTECTS AND NOURISHES ME"

Use this space to record how you plan on achieving a sense of wisdom in the future.

....

....

....

....

....

....

....

....

....

....

....

....

....

....

....

....

....

....

Hope

Humanity has always relied on hope. It is the light at the end of the tunnel, the one thing that encourages us to keep going. More than optimism, hope is true belief in a better and brighter future. When we look with hope, we see what could be. We imagine it in our minds, and then take positive actions to make it a reality. This is the natural order of hope. It motivates by offering a glimpse of the future as we would like it, and suddenly we can see a way forward. No longer is the world full of doom and gloom it is a place of potential and possibility, and we are filled with positive energy once more.

Before we know it, we're hooked on this feeling, believing that we deserve better and hoping for all our dreams to come true. While it may not be a magic wand, hope is a promise that things can change, and sometimes that's enough. A life without hope is flat and lacklustre, but with it, you'll find a vivid palette from which you can paint any picture.

This section looks at the power of hope and how you can create more of it in your life.

"HOPE IS THE PILLAR THAT HOLDS UP THE WORLD.
HOPE IS THE DREAM OF A WAKING MAN."
Pliny the Elder

**What are you hoping for in
your life right now?**

....

....

....

....

....

....

....

....

....

....

....

....

....

....

**What are your hopes for
the next month, year
and beyond?**

**If you're struggling to think
of anything, ask yourself
why. What is stopping you
from being hopeful?**

....

....

....

....

....

....

....

Your happy place visualization to
instil hope and optimism

Imagine you are perched on the brow of the hill. The damp grass prickles at your bare legs, but you don't care. It's going to be a beautiful day. You can feel it with every breath. There's a mist rising from the valley below. Swirling tendrils reach upward, as if they're trying to touch the clouds. It makes you feel like you are floating, suspended in mid-air.

Up ahead you see a glimmer of light peeking from the horizon. It's the soft glow of the early-morning sun rising. You watch as it gradually unfurls and light invades the landscape. The brightness it brings makes everything come alive. Colours become richer and shapes stand out, movement is amplified. Even the sound of the birds takes on new meaning. There is hope in this moment. A feeling that anything could and will happen. Slowly you rise to greet the sun, standing on your tiptoes, you stretch your arms upward and extend your spine.

You are infused with optimism, ready for anything, filled with hope.

"THERE IS HOPE IN EACH NEW DAY"

....

....

At what point in the
visualization did you feel
the most hopeful?

....

....

....

....

....

....

....

....

....

....

....

....

This happy place focuses
on the sunrise and the
beginning of a new day.
How do you feel when you
wake to a new day?

....

Identify one thing that you
could do to make you feel
more hopeful at the start
of the day, for example,
repeating a positive
affirmation or writing a list
of things to be grateful for.

....

....

....

....

....

....

"HOPE WILL NEVER BE SILENT."
Harvey Milk

One of the most hopeful sounds in the world is laughter. It brings people together and is full of joyous energy. When we laugh, we see and acknowledge the bright side. We take pleasure from the moment and our spirits are instantly uplifted. The ability to laugh at yourself and your situation has the power to transform your mood, and help you see that things can and will get better.

Think of the last time you had a really good laugh. Can you recall the moment and what caused it?

....

....

....

....

....

Identify and list at least five things that make you laugh from small things like watching your dog play, to big events, jokes and shows.

....

....

....

....

....

Consider how you can bring more laughter into your life.

"HOPE IS LIKE THE SUN, WHICH, AS WE JOURNEY
TOWARD IT, CASTS THE SHADOW OF OUR BURDEN
BEHIND US."
Samuel Smiles

If you've ever smelt the air after a sudden downpour, you'll know that rain has a distinctive aroma. Known as petrichor, this earthy fragrance occurs when raindrops touch dry soil. Rain is re-energising. The scent, along with the freshness, reanimates the landscape and imbues it with hope and colour. The next time you're caught in a rain shower, stop and take a moment to let the smell and feel of the rain renew you.

Rainwater washes away the dirt and makes everything shine. What can you wash away to restore a sense of hope? Identify the things in your life that you no longer need.

....

....

....

....

....

....

....

....

....

Draw a large circle and split it into sections that represent different areas of your life. Identify at least one thing that you can do to re-animate each area, for example, under career, you might put "get some training".

There is hope in emptiness. A blank canvas is an opportunity, a chance to create something new and exciting. While it's impossible to feel "nothing" in the literal sense of the word, when we're faced with the space to think and move freely, we leave room for hope to grow. We allow our imagination to fill the gap and manifest the things we want.

Pause, breathe and allow yourself the space to hope.

Think of this space as a blank piece of paper. Smooth down the pages and feel the potential.

What makes you feel hopeful right now? A new day, a rainbow, a certain piece of music? Make a list.

....

....

....

....

....

....

....

....

....

....

....

....

....

....

Most of the time we stumble through life, not really paying much attention to each new day and the potential that it holds. To increase hope, you need to switch your mindset and see the day ahead as an opportunity for greatness. This is easily done by embracing the day with a simple "greeting" that you can perform first thing in the morning.

It begins when you first get out of bed. Place your feet firmly on the floor and give yourself a minute to adjust to the feel of something solid supporting you.

1. When you're ready, slowly rise and stretch in any way you like.
2. Next, throw back the curtains/blinds and let the sunlight in. You might also want to open the window.
3. Draw a deep breath in from your belly and push your hands together in a prayer position.
4. As you exhale, push your hands upward to create a point above your head. Hold this position for a few seconds.
5. When you inhale, open your arms wide as if you're drawing a circle in mid-air, then bring them down to your sides.
6. Exhale, and let your chest soften. Imagine the light of the sun infusing you with positive energy.
7. Repeat these movements a few times, focusing on the breath, the stretch and inviting the sun's warming energy into your day.
8. To finish, make a positive statement like "I welcome this new day! I recognize the gift that this brings, and I am infused with hope."

How do you feel after the exercise? Did it make you
feel more hopeful about the day ahead?
Practise the exercise for a week, and then reflect on
any changes in your attitude and mood.

....

....

....

....

....

....

....

....

....

Pick out a highlight from each day. This can be
something that went well, a small success or a funny
moment. Write about it below, then reflect upon the
week and know that there is light to be found
in every moment.

....

....

....

....

....

....

....

....

....

your affirmation for **hope**

EACH DAY IS AN OPPORTUNITY, A GIFT, A TREASURE.

Use this space to record how you plan on achieving a
sense of hope in the future.

....

....

....

....

....

....

....

....

....

....

....

....

....

....

....

....

....

....

....

Loneliness and Isolation

Loneliness is defined as the state of distress or discomfort that we experience when there is a gap between our perceived level of social connection and our actual experience of it. Often mistaken for isolation, the two are not the same. A person can be surrounded by people and still feel lonely, just as a person who lacks social contact may not suffer from loneliness. Although the two concepts are different, they are interlinked. Those who are socially isolated can quickly become lonely, while those who are lonely will often withdraw and isolate themselves from others because they are depressed.

Who it affects

Loneliness is a state of mind that leaves sufferers feeling empty and unworthy of affection. They feel isolated and alone, and often crave contact, but because of a lack of self-esteem, they struggle to make connections with others. A recent global survey reported that around 33 per cent of adults experience feelings of loneliness throughout the world. While you might assume that a high number of these are elderly, evidence suggests that the young also suffer, with adolescents often feeling isolated from their peer groups, due to physical and emotional changes and the instability of social networks.

There is some evidence that loneliness decreases with the onset of middle age, and then starts to increase once again as we age, creating a U-shaped path as it rises and falls.

The effects of feeling lonely

Research shows that isolation and loneliness can lead to a number of health conditions including anxiety, depression, high blood pressure, heart disease, cognitive decline and Alzheimer's. Sufferers often develop bad habits to numb the emptiness they feel, and turn to alcohol, drugs and overeating, which in turn affects their general wellbeing.

Ways to feel connected

While bringing people together might seem the easy answer, particularly for those who feel isolated, it is not necessarily a long-term solution. The quality of the relationships you have is just as important as the quantity. To combat the loneliness epidemic we must work together and nurture our connections. Reaching out to friends and family, if only by phone or the use of a computer, is a great starting point, as is sharing thoughts and feelings. It also helps to get involved with the local community. Small things like a smile and snippet of conversation as you go about your usual routine can help you and the person you're taking to feel less alone in the world.

Balance

Life is a complex business, one minute up, the next down. It can be hard to maintain equilibrium, and yet it's something we need to remain composed. It's especially important in times of stress, when a sense of balance can help you feel safe, anchored and able to see the bigger picture.

Balance keeps us calm. It provides an inner strength from which we can face most challenges. It allows us a moment of respite so that we can detach, observe and then restore focus. When we feel balanced, we are not governed by our emotions. Instead we are steady and secure, supported by the earth and our environment.

For centuries, yogis have sought balance through meditation and other spiritual practices, and while it might seem hard to acquire, it is in fact a simple concept and something we are all capable of because it lives within us.

This section is all about finding the balance in your world and learning how to centre yourself.

"LIFE IS LIKE RIDING A BICYCLE. TO KEEP YOUR
BALANCE YOU MUST KEEP MOVING."
Albert Einstein

What makes it hard for you
to maintain your balance?
Identify the things that
knock you off kilter. For
example, a bad night's
sleep or a missed meal.

....

....

....

....

....

....

How do you centre yourself
during times of stress?

What kind of practices
do you think would
help to restore balance:
meditation, mindfulness?

Your happy place visualization to
help you find balance

You press your hands into moist soil. You can feel it part between your fingers as you mould a shape, a space from which your plant can grow. It's early in the morning and there's a freshness to the air, but you can also feel the sun upon the back of your neck, the promise of things to come. This plot of land is yours, a space for you to connect with nature and express yourself. You kneel and take a breath, feel the earth cradle you as you curl closer. You shut your eyes and imagine you're a shrub, a tiny sapling rooted to the ground. The hustle and bustle of the world can wait, for in this moment you are anchored. You have found your balance.

Gently you position the bulb so that it is nestled in the soil and then you cover it over, piling layer upon layer of soil, like a blanket. When you have done, you sit, your palms resting upon the surface of the earth.

Balanced. Measured. Rooted deep.

You have found your centre.

"I AM ANCHORED BY THE EARTH"

How did the visualization
make you feel centred and
close to earth?

....

....

....

....

....

....

....

....

....

....

....

....

....

Consider where you live,
your home and the people
around you. How rooted
do you feel?

How could you bring
more balance to your
environment? For example,
do you need to take
more time to practise
mindfulness?

....

....

....

....

....

....

....

> "BALANCE IS THE PERFECT STATE OF STILL WATER...
> LET THAT BE OUR MODEL. IT REMAINS QUIET WITHIN
> AND IS NOT DISTURBED ON THE SURFACE."
> Confucius

A soothing voice can be enough to restore a sense of balance. When we're feeling off kilter, hearing a loved one speak is all the medicine we need to centre ourselves. Even the voice of a stranger has the power to make you feel better, as long as it's calm and comforting. Lower-pitched voices are considered more grounding, particularly if the words spoken are slow but punctuated with meaning. Practise speaking in low, soothing tones, particularly when repeating affirmations. This should help you create a sense of balance.

Think about the people you know and also people you admire, and how they speak. Do they strike you as balanced or chaotic in the way they use their voice?

....

....

....

....

....

....

....

....

....

....

....

"HAPPINESS IS NOT A MATTER OF INTENSITY BUT OF BALANCE AND ORDER AND RHYTHM AND HARMONY."
Thomas Merton

Getting back to basics by doing things like planting in the garden can be enjoyable and grounding, particularly when growing your favourite blooms. Geraniums are flowers grown from bulbs that bloom in the height of summer. They are pretty to look at and also have a gorgeous uplifting scent, which is renowned for its ability to balance the emotions.

Introduce this lovely fragrance into your life. Burn a scented oil or add a few drops to bath water and immerse yourself in the aroma. However you enjoy the scent, close your eyes and let the sweetness calm and centre you. How do you feel?

Make a list of other plants and flowers to incorporate into your home that will help to give you a sense of balance.

....

....

....

....

....

....

....

....

....

Consider creating a scented flower garden to balance your mood.

Getting close to the floor and touching it with your entire body helps you feel supported, particularly if you're feeling shaky on your feet. It restores balance and also improves your inner core, which helps with posture. When you lay or stand with your spine aligned, you create a sense of balance in body and mind. You also see things from a different perspective.

Make a point of lying on the floor for a few minutes every day to recharge and regain your centre of balance. Pull your tummy muscles in and make sure your lower back touches the floor. Look up, look around. What do you notice? How does the space look different? Do you think it gives you a more balanced view of where you are?

Take your time getting to your feet and take a few deep breaths to steady yourself. How do you feel?

....

....

....

....

....

....

....

....

....

....

....

....

....

Balance is grounding. It brings you back to yourself and the present moment. It also opens up your awareness so that you can see the bigger picture.

The following mindful exercise will
help you feel more centred.

1. Set the intention to be more mindful when performing everyday tasks. For example, when you are making yourself breakfast, make it an exercise in mindfulness.

2. Absorb yourself in the preparation, from picking out bowls and plates to setting the table. Take your time over each action and really think about what you're doing.

3. If you're setting the table, think about the way it looks and how it complements the food you're about to eat.

4. If you're cooking something, like porridge, engage in the process. Focusing on the action of something simple like stirring can bring balance to your mind. If your mind wanders, take a deep breath and bring it back to what you're doing.

5. When you sit down to eat, connect with the experience by engaging your senses. How does your breakfast look, smell, taste? Savour the flavour and think of key words to describe it.

6. Finally, think about how it makes you feel. Eat slowly and pay attention to your stomach and when you feel full.

7. Know that the food you are eating provides sustenance, and will help to prevent energy dips throughout the day.

your affirmation for **balance**

WITH EVERY BREATH I FEEL MORE BALANCED
AND GROUNDED

Compassion

Compassion is the currency of kindness. It is a way to express your love and understanding, and it's something we all need in our lives. When times are tough and you are struggling, a caring word, a hug, a show of support can make all the difference and help you feel like you're not alone. Humans are social animals, we like to make contact with each other and form bonds, and compassion helps us do this.

It is the gel that keeps friends and lovers together, and it is born from empathy, from being able to put yourself in someone else's shoes and share their pain. When we act with compassion, we send a powerful message that says "You are not alone, I am here with you." Compassion, like love, is a two-way street, and while we might need it at some point, we also need to be able to show it to others, whether that's the people in our social circle, our community or further afield.

This section aims to help you develop kindness and compassion and share it with the world.

"NO ACT OF KINDNESS, NO MATTER HOW SMALL, IS
EVER WASTED."
Aesop

....

....

....

....

How compassionate are
you? Consider the areas of   ....
your life where you could
be more compassionate, ...
then make a list.
....

....

....

....

....

....

....

....

....   Think of five ways that you
could show compassion to
....   someone who is struggling.

....

....

....

....

Your happy place visualization to

help you find compassion

It's the heart of winter, and there is a chill to the air. You stand in the middle of a snowy landscape. A blanket of white covers everything. It is thick, icy and caked upon the earth. The sky is bright and heavy with snow. You can feel it pressing down, a spectral presence that takes your breath away. The trees point upward, stark and spindly, their branches seeking warmth. You draw a deep breath and feel your heart expand with love. Slowly you exhale, and as you let the air escape, the sky parts to reveal a glimmer of sunlight. The gentle rays bathe the earth in warmth, and you can feel nature respond to this gift.

Beautiful and bright, the sun casts its light, making everything sparkle. There's a feeling of empathy, as if the heavens have reached out with love and compassion. You smile because you feel it too, growing inside you. Your heart is open and ready to share. Compassion floods every part of your being and you let it flow out into the world.

With every breath, you understand more and your love shines brighter.

"EVERY DAY IS AN OPPORTUNITY FOR ME TO SHOW COMPASSION."

The visualization
illustrates compassion
through nature and likens
it to the warming rays of
the sun. When you show
compassion, how
does it feel?

....

....

....

....

....

....

....

....

....

....

....

....

....

....

....

....

....

....

....

....

List the days of the week
below, then write one way
you can show kindness
to someone each day,
for example sharing a
compliment, or words of
encouragement.

"THE DEW OF COMPASSION IS A TEAR."
Lord Byron

Music has the power to heal and touch the heart. When words just aren't enough or you can't think of anything to say, a melody or song that means a lot can bridge the gap and show your compassion. The next time you want to reach out to someone and show you care, try picking a song for them. You don't have to sing it unless you really want to! Simply choosing a song and sending it whichever way is easiest for you is enough.

Think of songs that mean a lot to you, that express love and compassion. Make a list below.

....

....

....

....

....

....

....

....

....

....

....

....

> "UNTIL HE EXTENDS HIS CIRCLE OF COMPASSION
> TO INCLUDE ALL LIVING THINGS, MAN WILL NOT
> HIMSELF FIND PEACE."
> Albert Schweitzer

Roses are synonymous with love. The pure, sweet scent lifts the heart, and the gesture of giving these beautiful blooms speaks volumes. Whether you're showing you care, expressing gratitude or simply saying "I'm here, I understand", the rose captures all this and more.

Show your compassionate side by treating someone to a bunch of these beautiful blooms or think of other ways to harness this uplifting scent, for example you could have a go at making rose water or take someone you love for a stroll in a rose garden.

Imagine "compassion" as a fragrance, what would it smell like?

....

....

....

....

....

....

....

....

....

....

....

Compassion is fuelled by empathy – the ability to feel what someone else is feeling, to be touched by their situation. Empathy comes naturally to some more than others, but the good news is it's a choice. We can decide to be more empathic in the way we relate to people, to allow their plight to touch our heart.

How empathic are you?
Think about a recent experience when someone you know was struggling with something. How did you relate to them?
Could you have been more empathic?

....
....
....
....
....
....
....
....
....

....
....
....
....
....
....
....
....

Identify three ways that you could show empathy and compassion, for example, listening more rather than trying to voice your opinion.

Compassion comes when we recognize that we are all connected. Everything we say and do has an effect on our environment. We can choose to create a positive atmosphere or a negative one, depending on our actions and our reactions. Nature works in harmony to create a seasonal cycle which benefits all things. We can do the same by taking inspiration from the natural world.

This exercise uses the power of nature
to help you harness compassion.

1. Find a plot of land, whether it's your own garden or a community garden, and use it to plant the seeds of compassion.

2. Start by assessing the condition of the soil. Do you need any extra compost? Is it nice and moist? Are there any weeds? This is about giving nature the best chance to blossom.

3. Once you have prepped the soil, think about what you're planting and what it needs to thrive. Some plants and flowers need lots of sunshine, while others prefer a shady spot. Plan your planting so that each plant gets the best chance.

4. Treat the time you spend on your patch as a type of meditation. Breathe and engage with every step of the experience.

5. Once you've planted and watered your flowers and plants, keep an eye on them. Check for weeds and other pests and water regularly. Also make sure you spend time in the garden, enjoying the space that you have created.

your affirmation for compassion

'I RELATE TO OTHERS WITH LOVE AND
UNDERSTANDING.'

Calm

A calm body and mind is the key to a happy, healthy life. The world is full of stress, from everyday pressures like balancing work and home life and all the demands that this brings, to worrying about finances and the bigger long-term picture – it's no wonder our minds are frazzled. When we suffer from stress, our bodies respond by producing hormones that increase our heart rate and blood pressure, causing us to feel even more anxious. If we can learn to relax and quieten the mind, we not only reduce the ill effects on our health, we can also learn to deal with pressure calmly and from a position of power.

Finding stillness in the chaos might seem like quite a feat, but it is possible if you're prepared to put the effort in. Calm, once found, is like a soothing river that flows through the body and mind and washes away all fear. It is a sanctuary that you can retreat to just by being more mindful and adopting an attitude of self-care.

This section aims to help you reach a place of peace, calm and tranquillity.

"WITH THE COMING OF SPRING, I AM CALM AGAIN."
Gustav Mahler

When do you feel at your calmest? Consider the environment and what you need to feel a sense of peace.

....

....

....

....

....

....

....

....

....

....

....

....

Identify and list all the things in your life that prevent you from feeling calm.

Come up with three things that you can do to help you feel calmer when you're stressed.

....

....

....

....

....

....

....

Your happy place visualization to
help you feel calm

Close your eyes and imagine you're standing on the shore. The golden beach stretches in every direction, and you breathe in the space. The bright blue sky is dotted with fluffy clouds and a seagull caws in the distance. The sound is sharp; it cuts through your mind and brings your attention to the horizon and the vast expanse of sea. Gentle waves roll toward you, their frothy white tips unfurling, as the water ebbs and flows.

On and on it goes, a constant motion driven by the tide. The ripples move outward in soothing patterns that eventually lap at your toes. You take a deep breath and draw in the sea air. It is salty upon your tongue. As you breathe out, you watch the ocean fall back to reveal the sandy beach once more.

You feel calm and centred.

All worries washed from your mind, seized by the waves.

It is just you and the perfect stillness of the sea.

"I FIND STILLNESS WITHIN ME."

What did you enjoy
the most about this
visualization? Which
aspects did you find the
most calming and why?

....

....

....

....

....

....

....

....

....

....

....

....

....

....

....

....

....

....

....

....

Can you recall a similar
experience or memory
when you were able
to spend some time
by the sea? Describe
the experience.

....

....

....

....

....

....

"THE SECRET OF SUCCESS IS TO BE IN HARMONY WITH
EXISTENCE, TO BE ALWAYS CALM, TO LET EACH WAVE
OF LIFE WASH US A LITTLE FARTHER UP THE SHORE."
Cyril Connolly

There is something soothing about the gentle rhythm of waves
and the ebb and flow of the water as it laps against the beach. It's
easy to get lost in the symphony of the sea, to imagine that you're
floating on the water, but if you struggled to recreate this during
the visualization, there are plenty of apps and online streaming
services that can help.

From bird song to raindrops against your
windowpane, make a list of the most soothing
noises in nature.

....

....

....

....

....

Think of a time when you were in nature and you felt
relaxed and at peace. Describe it here.
What made it so relaxing?

....

....

....

....

....

"EVERY BREATH WE TAKE, EVERY STEP WE MAKE, CAN BE FILLED WITH PEACE, JOY AND SERENITY."
Thich Nhat Hanh

Think about smells that remind you of being by the shore, the salty sea breeze, the fresh vibrant scent of seaweed and the aquatic aroma drifting up from the ocean bed. Try to recreate them in your mind.

If it helps, invest in ocean-scented candles or make your own sea salt room spray by adding 1 teaspoon of sea salt to a spray bottle and adding in 10 drops of fresh scented essential oil like lemon verbena. Top with water and shake well to mix, then spritz in the air and inhale the calm.

Identify and list other smells that remind you of the sea, things like sun cream or body oil, the sweet scent of ice cream.

....

....

....

....

....

Think of ways you can recreate these scents to help create the relaxing feeling of being at the beach.

....

....

....

....

....

From the cooling kiss of the water as it laps at your feet to the grainy softness of the sand, there is so much to touch and feel when you're beside the sea. It's a playground for the senses, and you can easily recreate the scene by seeking out textures that replicate this.

Put some tepid water in your bath and dip each foot in. Close your eyes and imagine you're paddling by the water's edge or sitting with your feet in the sea. Keep some shells nearby and explore their shape and the way they feel.

Identify other things that you can feel and touch that remind you of the seashore.

....

....

....

....

....

....

....

....

....

....

....

....

....

Go through your list and pick out the ones that make you feel calm.

One of the best ways to instil a sense of calm is with a breathing technique. When you're stressed out your heart rate increases and your breathing becomes rapid, which restricts the flow of air to your lungs. To think clearly and calmly you need to ensure you're getting enough oxygen. Deep breathing can help with this. It produces endorphins that help you relax and improves your general immunity. A breathing exercise will also focus the mind, and bring you back to the present moment when your thoughts are spiralling.

Find somewhere comfortable to sit, or lie down.
Close your eyes, and focus on your breathing.

1. Place both hands on your tummy so you can feel it move as you take each breath. Completely relax all your muscles and release any tension that you've been holding on to.

2. Take a long, deep breath in through your nose, and draw the air into your tummy; feel it fill your entire body.

3. Hold this breath for four seconds, then slowly release it through your mouth, counting out another four seconds.

4. Repeat this process, inhaling through your nose and holding for four long counts, then exhale through the mouth and make a swooshing noise as you release the breath.

5. Continue to breathe in this way for another minute, then when you're ready, take a deep breath in through your nose and count to five this time. As you do, imagine the oxygen reaching every part of your body, feel it soothing and clearing your mind.

6. Steadily release the breath through your mouth to the count of five beats.

7. Repeat this cycle again, holding and extending the breath for as long as you can, and continue with the exercise for another couple of minutes.

How did the breathing exercise make you feel?
Think about every part of your body and mind, and
write a few sentences.

....

....

....

....

....

....

....

....

....

Consider other ways that you could incorporate a
breathing technique into your daily routine: when
you need to feel calm, for example, you could make it
part of your morning commute to work.

....

....

....

....

....

....

....

....

....

your affirmation for **calm**

"EVERY BREATH HELPS ME FEEL CALM AND COMPOSED"

Use this space to record how you plan on achieving a
sense of calm in the future.

....

....

....

....

....

....

....

....

....

....

....

....

....

....

....

....

....

....

Compassion

The definition of compassion is that it is an emotional response to someone else's pain, which results in a genuine desire to help. While it is often confused with empathy, it is not the same thing. Compassion compels us to act and show love to others, it is often regarded as having sensitivity toward a person or a situation. Empathy is the ability to see and feel things from the perspective of another person, and in doing so, we might act compassionately, but we don't have to feel empathy to feel compassion.

The benefits

Scientists have discovered that compassion is a natural instinct, and an automatic response that has ensured the survival of the human race. It is something that brings us together, helps to build a common landscape and is the key to forming healthy relationships. It's also good for us. Research shows that when we act compassionately, our heart rate slows down, and the area of the brain associated with reward and pleasure is activated. Our bodies produce more oxytocin too, which in turn makes us feel good and actively encourages us to be even more compassionate.

Compassion at work

More recently, there's been evidence that suggests compassion is a key component of the workplace and results in a more productive environment. Acts of compassion among colleagues help to boost morale and also impact on the performance culture as a whole. In fact, compassion is cited as one of the top qualities required by leaders and those at management level, helping them to better understand and listen to employees.

Self-compassion and wellness

Self-compassion also plays its part in health and wellbeing. Research has proved that when we act with kindness and care toward ourselves, we build self-esteem and are less likely to suffer with mood swings or depression. We are also more likely to show compassion to others as we become less judgemental and more sensitive to the needs of different people.